The Chronically Disabled Elderly in Society

Recent Titles in
Contributions to the Study of Aging

The Chronically Disabled Elderly in Society

Merna J. Alpert

HV
1461
.A549
1994
West

Contributions to the Study of Aging, Number 24
Erdman B. Palmore, *Series Adviser*

GREENWOOD PRESS
Westport, Connecticut •London

Library of Congress Cataloging-in-Publication Data

Alpert, Merna J.
    The chronically disabled elderly in society / Merna J. Alpert.
        p.   cm.—(Contributions to the study of aging, ISSN
    0732–085X ; no. 24)
    Includes bibliographical references and index.
    ISBN 0–313–29109–8
    1. Frail elderly—Care—United States. 2. Chronically ill—Care—
United States. 3. Aged, Physically handicapped—Care—United
States.   I. Title. II. Series.
HV1461.A549 1994
362.4'0846—dc20   93–39351

British Library Cataloguing in Publication Data is available.

Library of Congress Catalog Card Number: 93–39351
ISBN: 0–313–29109–8
ISSN: 0732–085X

First published in 1994

Greenwood Press, 88 Post Road West, Westport, CT 06881
An imprint of Greenwood Publishing Group, Inc.

Printed in the United States of America

The paper used in this book complies with the Permanent
Paper Standard issued by the National Information Standards
Organization (Z39.48–1984).

10 9 8 7 6 5 4 3 2 1

This work is dedicated to Harry Alpert who, despite his own chronic health condition, expected excellence from himself and from those he loved.

Contents

Preface

The concept of the social complexity of chronic health conditions first developed in 1969 during the supervision of graduate social work students from the Adelphi University Graduate School of Social Work, who needed to have components of the three fields of social work in their first year internship. The unit was based in an acute care public hospital in a very depressed area of The Bronx, New York, in a neighborhood with all the social ills still prevalent today.

The sequelae of lead poisoning was selected as the focus of the student internship that year. Each of the students carried families with one or more children hospitalized with lead poisoning. One student organized tenants to redress physical deterioration in their building where a child had been hospitalized with lead poisoning. Another student worked with basketball players in a church basement to involve them in the problem. A hospital-wide interdisciplinary committee on lead poisoning was organized by one student, incorporating physicians, nurses, social workers, the demographer, and statistician. This committee wrote public letters in its own name, organized and conducted a borough-wide public meeting on lead poisoning, and responded positively to a request from a community activist organization to conduct two days of lead poisoning screening at their headquarters. A method developed in another university to test buildings for lead-based paint inexpensively was used by another student to involve volunteer community members. This plan was submitted to the city Department of Health. When an audience with the Commissioner of Health finally was secured, he preferred to use the sanitarians (only two at that time) for The Bronx to test buildings with Geiger counters! The student year ended on that note.

The students saw how the assignments of each contributed to mitigating a "real" community problem while helping individuals and families. The learning that took place that year was very exciting for all involved.

The next opportunity to develop the concept of the social complexity of chronic health conditions came in 1973, when the Hunter College Graduate School of Social Work supported the preparation of an in-house "Casebook on the Social Complexities of Chronic Disabilities" for its faculty under a training grant from the Social and Rehabilitation Service Administration of the Department of Health, Education, and Welfare. The casebook utilized two developmental and two degenerative health conditions.

In the spring semester of 1974, as an adjunct assistant professor, I taught the course on chronic health conditions at the Hunter College Graduate School of Social Work, opening the course to students of other graduate schools within the college. A few in dance therapy took advantage of this opportunity. The class was divided into teams which selected their own disease of interest. Each team member focused on and shared with the class one aspect of the social problems encountered. The broader understanding and awareness of the students about the disease studied was tremendous.

I was unable to continue work on this theme until the opportunity presented itself as part of Dr. Erdman B. Palmore's monograph series in gerontology. It is hoped this work suggests an approach to any chronic health condition—physical, mental, or emotional—affecting any part of the body of any human being of any sex, age, race, or nationality. Furthermore, it is hoped that the reader will develop a new awareness of the needs of and resources available to the chronically disabled in our society.

Acknowledgments

I am indebted to the many people and organizations who have supported and helped bring this work to fruition. It was their interest, time given, and sharing of information that provided the examples used to illustrate the ideas proposed. The examples were chosen in many instances from among many, primarily for the variety and interdisciplinary work they represent. Some were very successful, others faltered, as in all of life's endeavors. I am grateful for all provided, even those with basic premises with which I disagree. Unless otherwise noted in the text, they are presented simply as various facets of people and organizations related to the social functioning of the disabled elderly with chronic health conditions.

First, the research librarians at the Center for Disease Control, Emory University Health Sciences Library, and Georgia State University Research Library aided my search through the literature to ascertain whether or not this approach had already been developed. No similar works were found.

In the area of cognitive disability, I am grateful for the support given by Carolyn French, former Executive Director, and Janice Coye, Registry Director, both of the Atlanta Area Chapter of Alzheimer's Disease, for opening their library, sharing their grant applications, and introducing family care givers to me, and for their encouragement. Cathy Berger, Coordinator of Planning for the Atlanta Regional Commission, Aging Division, was most helpful with resources. Barbara Vahaba, Director of the Weinstein Adult Day Care

Center of the Atlanta Jewish Community Center permitted group interviews and opened agency records. Special thanks are due to Dr. Paul Cotten, Executive Director of the Boswell Retardation Center in Sanitorium, Mississippi, for sending samples especially written for this work. Many thanks are due to Miriam Pass Botnick for sharing her experience of developing and running a self-help group of care givers, Coping with Aging, for six years. The State Office of Aging through Fred McGinnis, Executive Director, Allan Goldman, Assistant to the Director, and other staff there and David Lee, Senior Policy Analyst, Senate Legislature, were most helpful in making available all material from the Alzheimer Study Committee to provide the examples of interdisciplinary involvement leading to governmental action and influencing legislation for long-term care insurance.

For hearing disability, the Superintendent of the Atlanta Area School for the Deaf, Mona McCubbin, and social worker Marcia Samuels Gitter, LMSW, made available their library, which provided some background, and the material and experience related to the proposal for a community service center. They also were most helpful in steering me to the Auditory Education Center, where Ellen Rhoades, Executive Director, opened their extensive library to me and encouraged two of their clients to provide contrasting examples. Cindi Lynn, audiologist at this center, is thanked for sharing her textbook to enhance my understanding of this problem.

In the area of motor disability, I am indebted to Dr. G. Fletcher, Executive Director, Dr. Michele Rusin, Dr. Bhoomkar, and Mr. Millgard, Administrator of the Emory Center for Rehabilitative Medicine, for enabling me to review records, sit in on staff meetings and a family conference; and review the history and administration of this facility. I wish to thank Mrs. Pat Szucs, Executive Vice President of the Visiting Nurses Association of Metro Atlanta for permission to review and use closed agency records. I also am indebted to Janet Sugarman, Director of the Louis Kahn Group Home, for sharing records and permitting individual and group interviews. Ms. Joyce Robinson and Billie Greenwell of the Regional Office of the Administration on Aging were most helpful in the way they made the compendium of active grants available.

Mr. Stanley L. Miller, Deputy Insurance Commissioner, Policy Forms Division, Office of the Commissioner of Insurance, and Ms. Smith were very helpful with their information on health maintenance organizations within Georgia. I also wish to thank United Healthcare Corporation and the Kaiser Foundation of Georgia, for sharing information on their respective health maintenance organizations. Special thanks go to all who shared with me the pain of their experiences with chronic health problems.

I wish space were available to thank the many other individuals and organizations who cooperated in my endeavors and enhanced by understanding, even though it was not possible to use their contributions due to space limitations.

I owe much to the three people who have reviewed and commented on this work to provide deeper insights and provocative thinking for me. They are Marian Glustrom, Assistant Professor of Sociology and consultant for many community projects involving older adults; Allan Goldman, Assistant to the Director, State Office on Aging, and Adjunct Assistant Professor in Public Health at Emory University; and Dr. M. Leah Gorman, Professor in the School of Nursing at Emory University. It was Leah Gorman who encouraged me to start this undertaking, and she was instrumental in holding my focus. She also was helpful in resolving many of the difficult questions that arose along the way.

Three people were instrumental in bringing this work to fruition. Two extraordinary people, Frances and Joe Lupton of Digital Sales, brought me from a manual typewriter to use of the computer. They both supported me through the arduous learning process and were available whenever I needed more help. I also want to thank Cornelia K. Bennett, whose expertise in APA style and typing ability made this work professionally acceptable for printing.

I wish to make it clear that I take full responsibility for questions raised and implications drawn from examples. The views expressed and any errors belong to the author and should not be attributed to the persons and organizations whose assistance was solicited, unless otherwise noted in the text.

One additional comment: Although most of the examples come from Georgia, the processes and concepts elucidated can be applied to other areas throughout the country with regional variations. If so construed, this work can be useful wherever there are caring people concerned about the problems of chronic health conditions.

The Chronically Disabled Elderly in Society

CHAPTER I

Introduction

The major purpose of this work is to increase public awareness and knowledge of problems of societal living among the chronically disabled elderly, as one effort to dispel commonly held stereotypes and dependency patterns. This is accomplished by focusing the material on four points: The first demonstrates that ramifications of chronic disabling health conditions among the elderly impinge on many facets of society. The second emphasizes that there is a pressing need for interdisciplinary collaboration to enhance the optimal functioning of the disabled elderly. The third shows that chronic conditions impact on the public sphere of societal health care and social services. The fourth is to raise the level of consciousness of policymakers, faculty members, politicians, administrators, and managers who make decisions affecting health care and social policy for the elderly with disabilities.

The foci listed above can be taught to all students in a manner that helps them retain their specialized focus. At the same time, this method includes the importance of other specialties and disciplines in the comprehensive care of older people with disabilities. Physical and mental/emotional chronic problems of older people cannot be divorced from the family or society.

MAJOR FACTORS INFLUENCING THE NEED FOR THIS WORK

Partial responsibility by a variety of medical and health care disciplines limits the effectiveness of comprehensive and continuous care (Illsley 1981: 327–330). The financial costs of health care needed on a long-term basis, sometimes intermittently, by those with chronic conditions has become overwhelming for insurance carriers and for governmental bodies, as well as for individuals and families.

Factors influencing life expectancy are well documented. These include control of many contagious and infectious diseases (Rosen 1958: 336; Sidel & Sidel 1977: 44–46), the explosion of medical knowledge, which prolongs life (Bonner 1974: 1–2; Illsley 1981: 327–330), and the more recent awareness of the need for individual healthy life-styles (Sidel & Sidel 1977: 290–291; Naisbitt 1982: 133–134). All of these factors, as well as twentieth-century developments in health care and technology, have served to prolong the life span, including that of those with severe and degenerative medical problems (Illsley 1981: 327–330; Roemer 1982: 122; Neugarten 1983: 390–392). Increased longevity with frequent accompanying chronic illnesses and disabilities poses a different kind of challenge to those medical specialists who have been indoctrinated to healing and curing (Rosser & Mossberg 1977: 88; Brown 1978: 60–68). Patients with chronic disabling problems have more need for intermittent and open-ended care for maintenance of functional ability (Sidel & Sidel 1977: 45–46).

Complex societal factors also have influenced the need for a comprehensive approach to chronic disabling conditions. The growth of the health care industry, which needs to make profits (Brown 1978: 66–68; Califano 1986: 210–212; Stoesz 1986: 246–248), and the increasing incorporation and privatization of health care, which tends to decrease the number of philanthropic community and public hospitals (Leyerle 1984: 163–164; Ginzberg 1985: 191–192), are important areas demanding public awareness. The high cost of sophisticated technology favors the growth of hospital chains and the demise of smaller hospitals. Thus, selective admissions based upon clinical interest and financial status prevail, depriving many potential patients of needed care, often not available elsewhere (Leyerle 1984: 163–164; Califano 1986: 210–212). In 1992 health care consumed nearly 13 percent of the gross national product. At the same time, patients without health insurance or other means of payment are being denied service in all but public hospitals (Leyerle 1984: 23, 151; Stoesz 1986: 248). The comparative lack of reimbursement by Medicare, Medicaid, and private insurance for intermittent long-term health care in non-hospital settings can be financially devastating to families (Rowland in Pepper Commission Report 1990: 125), yet long-term intermittent care frequently is necessary for the chronically disabled to maintain functioning ability (Sidel & Sidel 1977: 46; Illsley 1981: 328).

For the most part, public services to the elderly and disabled have financial caps and policy limitations based on limited assets and client age. Private agencies often add religious and/or ethnic eligibility factors. Staff shortages, lack of funding for community outreach, and lack of appropriate transportation denies services to some in need and to others who are unaware of the services. The tradition of philanthropic social casework and social group work (community centers) has been to provide services primarily to children, adolescents, young adults, and older able-bodied adults. Some social service agencies traditionally have serviced "their own," such as organizations providing services for the blind, the hard of hearing, the retarded, or those with cerebral palsy or Alzheimer's disease. Some of the specialized agencies have adhered to age-related eligibility, which effectively bars adults.

Home health care has been the traditional domain of visiting nurses associations and official public nursing agencies. Recent innovations in hospital cost containment and prospective payment systems have created a new expanding market for private home health care agencies. Diagnostic related groups (DRGs) in particular are forcing early discharge of patients who may need more medical care. The type of care needed by the patient discharged early, particularly those who are elderly and living alone, varies dramatically from basic housekeeping services to high-tech nursing care (Rinke 1987: 330–333; Griffith 1986: 301–302). Increasingly, hospital chains and medical supply houses are seeking a share of the home health care field, introducing a cadre of new workers such as technicians and case managers, some of whom may be poorly trained and have limited perspectives of the everyday needs of the convalescing chronically ill or disabled elderly. "The corporations need to show profits from their involvement, which often come at the expense of services needed by the chronically disabled elderly" (Trager 1986: 4–8).

The interdependence of medical and social factors in chronic and disabling health conditions is well documented (Illsley 1981: 327–330; Kahn 1985: 12–15; Simon 1979: 99–102). Illsley used the term "dependency groups" to include the handicapped, the chronically sick, retarded children, and the aged because they share similar characteristics, such as having conditions less amenable to curative treatment than to ameliorative treatment and, therefore, are professionally uninteresting. All are long-term users of resources and manpower and are not the clear responsibility of any one professional or service organization.

The interrelatedness of effects of various disabilities despite discrete and different causes has its counterpart in scientific research into the factors of one disease that have been found to affect other diseases (Kahn 1985: 12–15). For example, the effect of motor disability, which can arise from a number of different causes, may require similar adaptations in one's life-style, home, and the wider social environment for adequate functioning. This book focuses on the social effects of the health problem.

The number of noninstitutionalized people in the United States over age sixty-five with disabilities has climbed to many, many thousands. The best estimates of the number of noninstitutionalized older people with disabling conditions are found in the National Center for Health Statistics, National Health Interview Survey (1991: Series 10, No. 184), which are based on responses to selected representative subsamples of chronic conditions, including most of the disabilities of concern in this work. Cognitive dysfunction and mental retardation are omitted from the statistics in the NHIS material (noted in their Appendix 111, pp. 143–212). Also, "Totals for all chronic conditions are not shown because NHIS does not measure the total number of chronic conditions for each person. . . " who "may have more than one chronic condition" (p. 5). Tables 1.1 and 1.2 have been extrapolated to show only those health problems of interest here.

The above factors, which indicate the need for this work, result in societal complications which need to be addressed if a rational approach to health care and social services is to be developed for the disabled elderly to function at optimum ability in the least restrictive setting.

FOCUS AND ORGANIZATION

Only three disabilities are studied here. Cognitive disability is limited to Alzheimer's disease and mental retardation as examples of

Table 1.1
Number of Selected Reported Chronic Conditions by Age, United States, 1991 (in thousands)

Type of Chronic Condition	65 Years and Over		
	Total	65–74	75 and Over
Arthritis	14,666	7,768	6,897
Gout and gouty arthritis	881	499	382
Hearing impairment	9,710	4,780	4,839
Tinnitus	2,496	1,745	751
Absence of extremities (excluding tips of digits)	511	295	216
Paralysis of extremities, partial or complete	424	151	273
Deformity or orthopedic impairment	5,377	3,059	2,318
Deformity of lower extremities	2,227	1,250	1,977
Cerebrovascular disease	1,909	1,066	844

Note: Data are based on household interviews of the civilian noninstitutionalized population (extrapolated from Table 62, pp. 94–95, National Center for Health Statistics, Current Estimates from the National Health Interview Survey, 1991, Series 10, No. 184 USDHHS, Public Health Service, Centers for Disease Control, Hyattsville, MD, U.S. Government Printing Office, December 1992.

differing causative factors of cognitive problems. Adult onset hearing disability is utilized because of its prevalence. Motor disability is limited to the sequelae of arthritis and cardiovascular accidents, although it too can have many different causative factors occurring at any age.

Each chapter focuses on one chronic disability in its micro and macro contexts. Examples are used wherever possible to highlight actual experiences and processes. They may include portions of personal interviews, case records from health care and social agencies, reports from committees, sections of grant funding requests, educational training curricula, and reports of organizations and/or current laws. Examples were selected for their diversity and for their involve-

Table 1.2
Number of Selected Reported Chronic Conditions per 1,000
Persons by Age, United States, 1991

Type of Chronic Condition	65 Years and Older		
	Total	65–74	75 & Over
Arthritis	484.8	425.6	575.1
Gout and gouty arthritis	29.1	27.3	31.3
Hearing impairment	320.5	266.2	403.6
Tinnitus	82.4	95.3	62.6
Absence of extremities (excluding tips of digits)	16.9	16.1	18.0
Paralysis of extremities, partial or complete	14.0	8.3	22.6
Deformity or orthopedic impairment	177.5	167.1	193.3
Deformity of lower extremities	73.5	66.3	81.5
Cerebrovascular disease	63.0	58.2	70.4

Note: Data are based on household interviews of the civilian noninstitutionalized population (extrapolated from Table 57, pp. 82–83, National Center For Health Statistics, Current Estimates from the National Health Interview Survey, 1991, Series 10, No. 184 USDHHS, Public Health Service, Centers for Disease Control, Hyattsville, MD, U.S. Government Printing Office, December 1992).

ment of more than one professional discipline and/or agency. Questions are raised in appropriate sections of each chapter to elicit thinking about the help provided and societal ramifications of the material presented. The final chapter deals with implications and issues raised by the examples and related questions. It is hoped readers will raise even more questions and begin to search for potential solutions to the clinical, ethical, financial, and political issues related to chronic disabling health problems of the elderly.

Figure 1.1, Interrelationships Between the Disabling Condition and Selected Social Factors, is the basic plan. The material in each

Figure 1.1
Interrelationships Between the Disabling Condition and Selected Social Factors

section focuses on the functional ability or disability of the individual rather than on the medical diagnosis of the problem. The diagram projects visually that the disabling condition affects societal factors just as the latter affect and influence the disability of the individual. Examples are used wherever possible in order to illustrate these relationships. Other disabilities, such as lack of vision and manual dexterity, are not included due to space limitations.

The sections on government are not always appropriate examples, as used in this work. Therefore, other appropriate governmental material is presented. Health insurance as financial involvement usually is not specific to a particular disability. Therefore, the different types of health insurances are explored. Wherever feasible, the insurance sections cover information appropriate to the disability under discussion.

Parenthetically, it should be noted that the diagram will need other sections, such as education, heterosexual development, training for employment, and marital and family life, if it is utilized for developmental disabilities. Community and environmental factors in this work are an integral part of the examples used, particularly noted in family relationships, peer relationships, and activities of social functioning.

SUGGESTED USES FOR THIS WORK

This work has implications for educational institutions in the health and social sciences fields both didactically and for internships, limited only by the creativity of the faculty and students and the resources available. There are implications also for policy-making bodies, planners, administrators, and practitioners in health care and social services. Specifically, such professionals might plan, organize, and collaborate *with each other* and with self-help or support groups on policies, programs, and services for those with chronic disabling conditions. This may require a change of focus.

Additionally, this work might be a stimulus and aid to self-help groups in their organizing and advocacy efforts. Individuals and families might be more effective advocates on their own behalf after becoming more aware of the interrelationships among societal factors affecting their health problems and the need for collaboration with other groups.

Predictions for the future indicate continued increases in chronic health problems among the elderly (Olson, Caton, & Duffy 1981: 1–2). Therefore, it is vital that policymakers and decision makers in the gerontological, health, and social service industries press forward with integrated and comprehensive policies and practices to address this shift in population demographics.

"A society's quality and durability can best be measured by the respect and care given its elderly citizens" (Arnold Toynbee, historian, In *ADRDA Newsletter,* n.d.).

CHAPTER 2

Cognitive Disability

Cognitive impairment in the elderly is misdiagnosed more frequently than most other diseases of older people because symptoms are similar to and sometimes are exacerbated by those of other diseases. Under such circumstances the dementia is reversible when the disease is treated. Currently, there is no absolute way to estimate how many older people are affected by cognitive disorders. Cumulative inferential data suggest that 10 to 25 percent of all people over age sixty-five with cognitive impairment have *unrecognized treatable* diseases. There is general agreement in the literature with these findings (Beck et al., 1982: 235; Besdine 1982: 98, 112; Black & Paddison 1984: 42; Pedigo 1984: 139, 150–151; Glassman 1980: 288).

Emotional and psychiatric difficulties, especially if not treated correctly prior to old age, continue into the later years. Many difficulties in later life may have roots in one's early development, but they may remain dormant or latent until there are failing societal supports such as death of family members, lack of employment, or deteriorating physical abilities or senses. In old age emotional and psychiatric conditions rarely occur separately from physical problems and often may be difficult to isolate. Even today many physicians tend to overmedicate older people without having a full diagnostic workup, a full psychosocial history, a full medical history, or a full understanding of the effects and side effects of a "normal adult dosage" on older people, thus causing iatrogenic disorders (Wolfe

1989: 1–6; Besdine 1982: 98; Glassman 1980: 289–290). This work uses Alzheimer's disease (AD) and mental retardation (MR) as examples of cognitive disability.

Alzheimer's disease usually develops among mature and older people due to deterioration of specific parts of the brain. Mental retardation has been attributed both to genetic factors, and therefore is immutable, and to environmental factors, and therefore is malleable (Zigler 1988: 4). Today retarded people often outlive their care-giving parents (World Health Organization, Offset Publ. No. 86, 1985: 37). This work examines the effects of both these problems on the lives of and in the social fabric related to older people.

Alzheimer's disease is a degenerative condition with a progressive decline in intellectual, social, behavioral, communicative, and physical functioning abilities. Changes seen microscopically include abnormally large numbers of structures called neuritic plaques and neurofibrillary tangles. There are many avenues of research into possible causes, including somatic, viral, genetic, and environmental theories. No specific cause has been found yet. Eventually, the patient needs complete physical care. This process can take from one to twenty years (Mace & Rabins 1981: 223–231).

Mental retardation is an example of a developmental disability also presenting cognitive problems in later years. Prior to the "open door" policy of deinstitutionalization, many mentally retarded lived in institutions. The trend today is to help those who can to live in the community. Those who live with their families now may outlive their parents. Therefore, greater numbers now are coming to the attention of the formal system of social services and to aging services (Rose & Janicki 1986: 15).

Mental retardation "involves two essential components: a) intellectual functioning that is significantly below average, and b) marked impairment in the ability of the individual to adapt to the daily demands of the social environment. Both factors must be impaired before a person can be considered to be mentally retarded. Neither alone is sufficient" (WHO, Publ. No. 86, 1985: 37). However, impaired intellectual functioning can influence impaired social functioning.

The IQ level generally has been used to designate different degrees of handicap for each retarded individual. In 1985 the World Health Organization accepted the following classification:

Level of Retardation	IQ Level	% of Retarded
Mild	50–70 or 75 ⎫	75%
Moderate	35–50 ⎭	
Severe	20–35	20%
Profound	0–20	5%

This work focuses on those who can and do live in the community: primarily the mildly retarded. The total number of people who are retarded is unknown. (This term is used throughout because the current label of "developmentally disabled" applies to people of all ages who may have other chronic health problems without being mentally retarded.) However "it has been estimated there are between 200,000 and 500,000 older adults nationwide with a 'developmental disability.' This means that about 4 out of every 1,000 older adults have a 'developmental disability'" (Rose & Janicki 1986: 15).

"There is a great deal of variability of behavior among individuals who have similar IQ levels related to their individual development" (Rose & Janicki 1986: 18). However, Zigler's review of H. H. Spitz's book is somewhat more explicit. Zigler points out:

> there is a subgroup of retarded individuals who have been demonstrated to have some organic abnormality. . . . The remaining half . . . have no known organic factor underlying their retardation and thus represent one of the greatest mysteries in psychology. The developmental formulation of mental retardation includes the tenet that . . . performance on any task is not determined by the individual's cognitive capacity alone, but also reflects a number of motivational and personality factors . . . which are the result of the particular histories of the retarded individuals. . . . We probably cannot train retarded persons to be more intelligent, but we can improve motivation and teach greater social competence. (1988: 9)

Keeping that in mind, we are reminded that

> Developmentally disabled elderly citizens share many of the same medical conditions and impairments, and have many of

the same chronic health problems as other older people. . . .
There is a great confusion regarding the difference between
long-term mental illness and the developmentally disabled as
both populations age. People with developmental disability also
have mental health needs. (Rose 1988: 3)

EFFECTS ON THE INDIVIDUAL

The observed effects of Alzheimer's disease and mental retardation
on the elderly comes most often from those involved in the care-
giving role, because an individual with cognitive disability most often
is not aware of or cannot verbalize the problems, as the examples
below will indicate. The exception to this rule of thumb is the person
with beginning Alzheimer's disease.

The following sequence, taped in a 1987 group interview at a senior
adult day care center, shows one person's struggle to verbalize her
understanding about the disease. This woman had been a probation
officer in another state and was brought here by her son when it was
felt she could no longer live alone. She said she has some medical
difficulties, which is why her son wanted her to come to this city.
"Do you want to know why I'm coming [to the center]? It is because
I have Az, Az, Az. Now it's showing because I am getting nervous."
She decided to write the name instead. "I think I have the name of
it now, Azenheim. I'm not pronouncing it right. I don't think I've
ever really had it. If I do have it, I'm working on it the proper way.
I'm getting better."

Later in the interview, she shared the following: "It's scary because I
may be regarded as playing tricks on somebody." She then gave an account of a lengthy conversation she recently had had with a physician
who, she said, didn't expect her to maintain a lucid conversation. She
ended with the statement: "I'm talking to you now because I haven't
any fear." Her fear seemed to relate to being considered "wrong" and
subject to correction by others. The staff at the center said that this
woman, although previously informed of her disease, had never been
able to utter its name or admit that she had this problem.

A very informative and poignant account of the meaning of Alzheimer's disease to the affected person and his family is provided
by Lyons (1982: 3–20), who includes his understanding of the difficulties, feelings, and fears of the person with Alzheimer's, as well as

the family care giver's understanding, feelings, and fears. Lyons's account and this author's professional experience indicate the need for care-giving others to try to follow the "ramblings" or "ravings" of the cognitively impaired until they are less troubled by their confusion. This may be initially more time consuming, but it makes subsequent encounters easier for both. Often seemingly irrational verbalizations are rooted in some aspect of life history and/or emotional relationships. This emphasizes the need for psychosocial histories as thorough as possible for older people, especially for those with cognitive disability.

Examples of the effects of mental retardation on the individual are more difficult to obtain. The actual condition remains relatively stationary, although functional effects can be enhanced or lessened through sensory, intellectual, and/or environmental stimulation (Zigler 1988: 6). Each retarded person differs from others, dependent on life history and stimulation, the responsiveness and reactions of others in the environment, as well as on innate intellectual and functional abilities. Janicki (1986: 4) points out that older retarded people can be categorized into three sections. The first section represents those older persons who have been fairly independent all their adult lives and now need special assistance because of aging problems. The middle section represents those who are moderately mentally or physically impaired, are the potential users of day care services and special assistance programs. The third section represents the more severely mentally or physically impaired who have been the lifelong responsibility of the developmental disabilities system and will continue there.

A group interview at the adult day care center included one man in his seventies who was known to be retarded. The agency record indicated the following social history: Nothing of his family life and childhood was noted except that he reached the ninth grade in school and seemed good at spelling. No family seemed to be nearby. He never married. He attended the Department of Family and Children's Services (DFACS) training center. For all of his working life he sold newspapers in the lobby of an office building. He lives alone in public housing for the elderly. For many years a DFACS worker has been his primary care giver and helped him manage money, which he could not do effectively. In 1977 his IQ on the WAIS scale was sixty-five, with performance at fifty-eight and verbal at seventy. Mr. B.'s physical problems included bronchitis, phlebitis, and circulatory problems due to varicosities. He is "addicted" to cigarettes and coffee. In 1983 he suffered a cardiovascular accident and also had prostrate surgery. He was discharged home with help from visiting nurses. After this, he was referred to the center for socialization, exercise, and monitoring of his medications and smoking and eating habits.

A psychological evaluation when Mr. B. was sixty-six years old found him to be oriented in all spheres with a "childlike geniality" and verbal responses that "flitted." When he was asked to return to a task he "grinned sheepishly like a child who forgot." It also was noted that he exhibited "excessive jocularity" and had frequent "myoclonic jerks of unknown origin." Mr. B. taught himself to play the harmonica by ear and bought himself a new one every Christmas.

At the start of the group session Mr. B. began playing his harmonica. He put it away only after he was promised we would welcome his playing for the tape at the conclusion of the discussion. During the discussion his speech, in response to questions, seemed mumbled, making it difficult to understand him. He did not generate any comments or questions of his own volition—with the exception of frequent questions about the cleanliness of his clothing and worry about where his keys were. His responses and manner of relating cannot be generalized to other people with similar classifications.

One cannot but wonder whether, with his interest in and good ear for music, Mr. B. could have been encouraged and helped to develop his talent in this area. Might this have made any difference in his other social skills? Can the woman who formerly was a probation officer maintain some kind of connection with her field of service? These questions hint at sensitive listening and creative and innovative ways to help disabled elderly with cognitive problems maintain contact with their more successful selves as long as possible. The questions also indicate that more could be done by families, neighborhoods, communities, and the formal service agencies to provide understanding, space, time, and meaningful activities and opportunities for these types of disabled people. Senior adult day care centers, especially those under the sponsorship of the Alzheimer's Association, with staff and volunteers trained for this work, have made great strides in this direction.

EFFECTS ON FAMILY RELATIONSHIPS

When any family member—spouse, parent, child, or sibling—becomes cognitively impaired, the effects on the family as a cohesive functioning unit undergo important structural changes. The balance previously achieved within the family needs to change; emotional relationships and support undergo transformation; activities of social functioning usually are curtailed (Kerson & Kerson 1985: 277, 279, 281; Shaw 1987: 408–409; Silverstone & Hyman 1976: 42–45; Mace & Rabins 1981: 141–144, 148, 155–173; Lyons 1982: 3–20; Poe 1969: 30–31, 48–49, 52–53); and income may be reduced and financial resources used up by new and ongoing expenses (Weiler 1987: 1157–1158). When a parent or spouse is cognitively impaired there is need for an emotional readjustment to the changed status, functional abilities of, and altered relationship to the deteriorating person. The complexity of the care giver's emotional need to adjust to and mourn the loss of "the person that was," while at the same time providing the needed care and support to "the person that is," is a very important factor influencing the quality and continuity of care giving (Shaw 1987: 407–408; Marples 1986: 492).

When the disability is developmental, as in retardation, the parents usually are the care givers who have special stresses. The perpetual parenting "never ends for many parents whose DD [sic] adult children, in their own feelings and words, never grow up. Theirs is a task of lifelong caregiving" (Jennings 1987: 430). "This task has both rewards and burdens for the care giver and both benefits and omissions for the retarded person" (Rose & Ansello 1987: 70–71).

The needs of care-giving relatives have been well documented in the literature (Poe 1969: 52; Silverstone & Hyman 1976: 15–61; Gross-Andrew & Zimmer 1978: 119–134; Zarit, Reever, & Back-Peterson 1980: 649–655; Weeks & Cuellar 1981: 388–391; Lyons 1982: 3–20; Bankoff 1983: 226–230; Stoller & Earl: 1983: 64–67). In particular, there are five care giver needs, in addition to financial support, which ought not to be overlooked by health care and social service providers. These are (1) the need for education about and understanding of the disability; (2) the need for recognition and acceptance from other family members, the community, and formal support systems; (3) the need for support, be it emotional, financial, and/or helpful skills and techniques; (4) the need for periods of respite without guilt; and (5) the need to have the ability to relinquish the care-giving role without guilt when it is appropriate (Alpert, 1983). Some of these needs can be met through participation in self-help groups.

In recent years such groups have proliferated among people who have a common bond. Examples are Alcoholics Anonymous and Alanon; veterans advocacy groups; Reach to Recovery; and self-help groups relating to specific diseases. Naisbitt (1982: 133) relates this phenomenon to the general feeling of being unable to control government and the distancing imposed by bureaucracies. This author would add the consciousness-raising of the women's liberation movement, which provided women the self-confidence to make decisions in areas hitherto denied them; and the civil rights movement spearheaded by Dr. Martin Luther King, Jr., which empowered its adherents to effect changes in established institutions of society.

Generally, self-help groups in the health field start by bringing "peers together for mutual assistance in satisfying a common need" (Naisbitt 1982: 150). The following example illustrates this.

An interview on October 25, 1987, with the director of Coping with Aging, a self-help group which functioned from 1979 to 1985, resulted in the following account. Coping with Aging was started after the director attended professionally sponsored, time-limited support and training groups because of her cognitively impaired parent. "But when the meetings were over my problems were still there." She developed an ongoing support group by securing limited financial support from a service organization and arranged for a meeting room on a regular basis in a community center to avoid perceived negative attitudes about hospitals, nursing homes, or casework agencies. There was some local publicity to announce the group and appropriate health care and social service professionals were alerted to this new resource for referrals. Later, word of mouth brought in new members.

The group met monthly for six years. Generally there were fifteen to twenty people present for support and help. Each meeting focused on one topic, which was addressed by an invited expert. Usually members suggested topics of concern for future meetings. The director made all the arrangements for each meeting. She called each participant on a monthly basis, between meetings, as well as each absent person. Additionally, she sent written meeting reminders. As important as the regular meetings was the personalization of calling and writing each member, which helped them feel "cared for." She also arranged for all the guest speakers and provided refreshments. The socialization at the end of each meeting enabled members to get to know one another, share some of their burdens, and express caring, which they did also by phoning each other between meetings. This self-help support group was the first in the city; by 1985 there were a number of ongoing support groups in the area established by the Alzheimer's Association (the AA), thus eliminating the urgency to continue this particular group.

Lyons (1982: 3–20) discusses at some length the effects of AD on care givers, especially on a spouse. He indicates there is shock, helplessness, and panic with the realization of a deteriorating disease which cannot be stopped. There is a need to understand the feelings of other family members who accuse the care giver of exacerbating the problem; to learn how to utilize offers of help in ways that provide a meaningful role for others; and to learn how to request needed help. It is crucial when accepting household help to learn how to interview and screen applicants, and to help the impaired person and the outside help to connect positively with one another. Other areas of importance include the importance of understanding all the side effects of medications and having a good working relationship with the physician (it is important for the patient to have a good physical checkup to discover if there is some irritation or organic problem causing the irrational behavior); dealing with neighbors, shopkeepers, and acquaintances who "look askance" and show pity or repugnance; and dealing with family and friends who visit in groups and do not realize the difficulty the patient has in following conversations, much less in participating. The care giver needs to learn to look for clues to understanding the causes of the words or behavior that seem irrational. It is important for the care giver to deal with the guilt and ambivalence about the need to relinquish the care-giving role and trust others, when necessary.

The effects of Alzheimer's disease on adult children differs somewhat from that of the spouse, as indicated in the following examples. An interview on December 9, 1987, with daughters of two Alzheimer patients highlighted the fact that their mothers, who previously had lived alone, came to live with them and their families.

Mrs. G.'s mother had been mishandling her finances, not cashing checks or paying bills, and was showing symptoms of paranoia. She fought any loss of independence, including coming to live with her daughter and loss of control over her money. Mrs. G. said that the care giver "needs to be sly and sneaky" to secure the necessary signatures when legal guardianship and financial control are needed. She also said, "It's hard on the care giver when it is necessary to take away the independence of your own mother." This occurred in 1979, when there were no family support groups available to her and the Alzheimer's Association (the AA) was not yet functioning in her city. Mrs. G.'s mother could not be left alone. Mrs. G. asked her sister, a schoolteacher, to relieve her two hours daily. The sister refused even that much help, but did arrange for Mrs. G. to do her shopping. Mrs. G.'s husband walked away from the situation as much as possible.

Mrs. G. and her husband had no knowledge of what was wrong with her mother in 1979.

> I took her to a psychiatrist to find out what was wrong and why she was behaving so irresponsibly. He prescribed Haldol and told me to expect a muscular reaction as the side effect. That didn't happen. She became a zombie, active twenty hours daily, up and down all the time. After two months of living like this we admitted Mother to a nursing home, where they took her off the medication. She had deteriorated so much that she had to be taught all over again how to use utensils to eat. If I had known then what I know now, things would be very different.

Mrs. G. still is involved with her mother through frequent visits and personal help. Her mother is sometimes in contact with reality, still plays the piano for others, and enjoys personal contact. Mrs. G. said she wanted to understand all this. She eventually joined a family support group, but she needed more. She went back to college and graduated. "My mother's sickness enabled me to know myself better and made a vast improvement in my life." She felt that the worst part of dealing with this sickness is the "absolute frustration of not knowing if you are doing the right thing for that person."

Mrs. A. explained that it was easy to help her mother at first, because she requested and relied on that help. Her mother finally had so much difficulty making decisions that the A.'s brought her to live with them. "We had her diagnosed before she came to live with us."

This occurred in 1982, and Mrs. A. was put in contact with the AA, which had started family support groups. This helped Mrs. A. to "understand my own feelings and cope with Mother's rages." She felt this was a very important support and learning experience for her.

Mrs. A. said she had a good support system in her grown children and husband. Despite this, there were tensions in family relations, such as how to handle her mother's aggressive outbursts. Mrs. A. noted these occurred regularly when her mother was rushed in order to keep up with the pace of family life. Mr. A. wanted to treat them with tranquilizers. With the physician's support, Mrs. A. successfully resisted this. However, Mrs. A.'s mother fantasized nightly that Mr. A. raped and impregnated her. To guard against this, nightly she took out linens to cover all the windows and doors. After this fantasy spilled into daytime conversations and fears, making communication very difficult, nursing home placement was considered. Mrs. A.'s mother still seemed amiable and lucid to the grandchildren, who were horrified about such placement. Mrs. A. then had her children care for their grandmother for a few days, which increased their understanding of the problem.

Mrs. A. said she learned through the support group that she had to "learn to let go, to give up. You have to let go the grief and get back to reality." She felt the greatest hurt occurs "when they know they have lost something and you want to give it to them and know that you can't." Mrs. A. recounted more recent incidents clearly indicating how hurt she still is that her mother no longer responds as a parent or grandparent.

The Lyons account of a spouse and the interview with the children show some of the emotional differences of family members. The partial loss of a spouse with whom one has lived for many years differs from the partial loss of a parent, especially when one also has other primary family.

Community resources in these examples clearly were related to the time element and "state-of-the-art" knowledge. The AA was just starting in 1979. Before then, Alzheimer's disease was considered "the silent epidemic" among those who knew of this disease. Support groups for care givers were being written up in the early 1980s (Cohen 1983: 248–250; Haber 1983: 251–253; Stafford 1980: 656–660). Those like Mrs. G. and Mr. Lyons, who had to live with this illness before then, did not have this resource available. Mrs. A. indicated, more than once, how important the support group had been to her understanding of her own feelings and coping with her mother. This disease, in particular, presents changes in the patient which require coping strategies by the care giver, who needs to adapt to the stages of the disease. The sense of sharing and helping developed in the AA family support groups is as crucial as formal education for the family care giver. The Lyons and Mrs. G. examples also indicate the need for physicians and other health care providers to cooperate or collaborate in their care of patients with degenerative diseases so that family care givers also can contribute appropriately.

The questions raised by these examples seem almost self-evident. Do social services professionals, exemplified by Lyons, feel they need less support because of their professional knowledge and understanding? His article indicates he had the same needs as nonprofessionals. How can professionals who are care givers be helped to connect with appropriate helpers? Should physicians prescribe psychotropic medications when they are not knowledgeable about the person's psychosocial history, medical history, physical status, and so on and when their knowledge of the disease is limited? Should family members accept a physician's recommendations without any understanding or questions? Should families seek responses and understanding from other specialists with other areas of expertise? What is the most appropriate and least expensive way for families without any knowledge of cognitive dysfunction to get an appropriate diagnosis? How can care givers, who may be medically illiterate, be guided to the appropriate entry point in the health care system? All health care providers and social service workers need to be able to refer families to appropriate available community resources, as many nurses and social workers do.

Ongoing support groups that benefit care givers directly should be extended to spouses, children, and other relatives to encourage mutual support instead of the miscommunication that often occurs when dealing with an Alzheimer's patient. The examples also highlight the importance for physicians to learn how to prescribe medications for older people to avoid iatrogenic reactions and especially to closely monitor psychotropic drugs. The examples underscore the need for care givers to question health care providers until the former understand what, why, and how to deal with the illness. These examples also clearly indicate the need to find available appropriate community resources.

No example of the effects of elderly retarded people on other family members were available to the author. With health care improvements, more and more retarded people now are outliving their parents. Formerly, the retarded person frequently was institutionalized because needed help was not available in the community (Rose 1988: 2–3).

The reader with an opportunity to view a television program called "Best Boy" will see elderly parents caring for a retarded son in his fifties. This very sensitive portrayal of family life with a retarded adult was one segment of a series called "Point of View," produced by WNET in New York, New York. It aired during 1988.

EFFECTS ON PEER RELATIONSHIPS

Alzheimer's disease has a marked effect on friends who knew the person before the disease was noticeable. Frequently the affected person's focus narrows to one topic, no matter what the subject of the conversation. Family and friends tend to become confused first, then irritated by the repetition. Efforts to change the topic of conversation may result in confusion in the patient, which may be followed by even more inappropriate behavior. Family and friends may give up trying to communicate as time goes on, thus isolating the person even more.

Another problem occurs when two or more people visit at the same time. The person with Alzheimer's tends to have difficulty following a conversation with more than one person at a time. The visitors gradually talk to each other and other family present, bypassing the sick person and thus leading to frustration. In essence, then, persons with this disease gradually become isolated from most friends who knew them previously. If family members do not make the effort to communicate, for whatever reasons, the isolation is further increased.

Another aspect of peer relationships among the cognitively impaired has received only minor attention (known to this author) in the professional literature. Friendships can be maintained or newly developed by "doing with" instead of "doing for"; by "listening to" and "talking with" instead of "telling" and "talking to." Many simple activities come to mind, some of which may need adaption for the satisfaction of the cognitively impaired as well as for the unimpaired person. Finding and providing opportunities for fun and laughter also is a great help in maintaining and developing positive peer relationships. All of these require extra time, effort, and creativity by both informal and formal care givers. The adult day care centers maintained by the AA are demonstrating the effectiveness of this technique.

According to the director of the Weinstein Adult Day Care Center, in a September 1987 interview, those with Alzheimer's participate in activities they can handle with others not cognitively impaired. These tend to be physical activities such as exercise sessions, active games, singing, taking walks, devotionals, and holiday celebrations. During other activities, such as movies, discussions, and table games, there are separate activities with staff members for each.

At adult day care centers sponsored by the AA, the whole program, with as many cooperative interactive activities as possible, is geared to various levels of Alzheimer's disease. These centers have a high ratio of staff (including volunteers) to participants for more individualized attention. The social effects of attending day care centers is noticeable to the staff. When "partners" are necessary, some select the same one each time. Some participants note the absences of others. The staff notes that positive interaction, verbal or physical, among the participants increases. Family care givers have commented on the positive effects of day care participation, such as more self-maintenance by the patient, more appropriate verbalization and responses, and a more calm demeanor (Van Tuyl 1987: 4–5).

An agency record noted that Mr. B., the retarded man, was seen as friendly and gregarious during more physical activities and while playing his harmonica. It pointed out he had difficulty concentrating on discussion, movies, and reminiscences. He had very limited ability to recall past events. His short attention span required the worker to help him stay with an activity. During the interview he said he enjoyed music, balloon volleyball, dancing, and seniorsize (an exercise program) at the center, but for the most part, he did not volunteer any conversation. The other group members had Alzheimer's disease and appeared neither to notice nor be irritated by his behavior. Yet, despite their own cognitive impairment, they sometimes reacted to and corrected each other.

Questions arise. Who are the peers of the cognitively impaired:

those who knew the person before the problem arose, those who have similar conditions, or possibly both? Are peers those of the same chronological age, the same intellectual age, or the same emotional and socially functional age? Should an Alzheimer's patient with a functional and intellectual age of five have frequent social contact with five-year-old children? Should the retarded older adult have primary contact mostly with other retarded older adults, especially since it now is known that social and intellectual stimulation enhances social adaptation in the retarded (Zigler 1988: 8)? The push for deinstitutionalization in the 1960s, for mainstreaming in education in the 1970s, plus advances in scientific knowledge have led to better understanding in this area.

Adult day care centers can help cognitively impaired people function as fully as possible, but such centers are not the only answer. Both progressive cognitive impairment and mental retardation do not preclude the possibility of helpful volunteer activity (as the example in the next section will show) and some participation in the general community. Much, much more can be explored and developed by informal and formal care-giving systems to integrate the cognitively impaired elderly into the general community, particularly if cooperative activities are planned and volunteers are used wisely.

ACTIVITIES OF SOCIAL FUNCTIONING

Activities of social functioning relates to activities usually performed with other people, such as attending and participating in religious activities, voting, eating in restaurants, using public transportation, participating in service organizations, attending cultural and sports activities, and participating with others in recreational activities. These are some of the social activities that enhance the quality of life for those of all ages, including older people. People will continue to make choices whenever possible, even in their mature years, usually from among those activities familiar to them from past experiences. Being involved with others in such ways helps to keep them connected to their own lives and can help to mitigate the tendency toward withdrawal and isolation. It also enhances physical well-being and may help to lessen depression, which often accompanies disability.

A national survey of programs serving elderly mentally retarded persons was initiated in 1984 (Krauss & Selzer 1986: 1–15). The purposes of this study were to collect and document information on what services were available in day programs serving this clientele and to provide recommendations for other agencies serving elderly retarded persons.

Highlights of this survey indicated fewer day programs than residential programs, 37 percent to 63 percent, whether they were based institutionally or in the community. The peak year for creation of day programs both in the community and in institutions was 1984. Day programs included, in decreasing numbers, vocational day activity programs, day activity programs, supplemental retirement programs, leisure and outreach programs, and senior citizens programs.

The survey concluded with special mention of the enthusiasm, depth of concern, commitment, and dedication of the staffs in these programs. Their common refrain was that adequate retirement programs were lacking, the participants' medical needs were too often not well served, staff needed more formal training about the aging process, and that more resources are needed to enrich the lives of clients.

It should be noted that newsletters of the National Alzheimer's Association and the local chapters have carried a number of articles providing tips for care givers on the value of social stimulation and how to develop such activities with the disabled.

People whose cognitive impairment progressively deteriorates have more difficulty maintaining activities of social functioning and usually need the help of others to continue. Mrs. G.'s mother, in a nursing home for seven years and often out of touch with reality, but still playing the piano for her own and other's enjoyment, is an example of a social activity that connects her to her past life. Mr. B., who continues to give himself an annual present of a new harmonica and plays for himself and others, is another example of staying connected to his earlier life. Sensitive care givers can build on such interests and abilities creatively to stimulate and/or enhance the weakened ego strengths of individuals. This takes time, planning, effort, and imagination by the care givers, whoever they may be.

If Mr. B.'s support system can be generalized to other people, certain questions arise. His primary care giver is his caseworker from the Department of Health and Human Services. She helped him manage his financial matters and referred him to the day care center.

How many changes of caseworkers did he have over the years, with different personalities, different capabilities, differing levels of interest in him, and functioning within different agency parameters? How many of his caseworkers were concerned about the quality of his life, as well as with his health and money management? Did any of his caseworkers encourage his interest in the harmonica or music in general? Was his retirement from his lifelong work prepared for or planned in any way? Was there any attempt to involve any other person or organization with him in any way? The answers to these questions for Mr. B. are unknown, but hopefully the parameters of public and private agencies can expand to encompass such functions and provide personnel to carry them out. Professional satisfaction in helping clients to function at higher levels may help to lessen staff burnout and high rates of staff turnover.

The example for this section is that of a man who lived in an institution for the mentally retarded for fifty years. He was deinstitutionalized successfully at age seventy-three. (This was contributed via written communication in June 1988 by Dr. Paul Cotten, F.A.A.M.R. Director of the Boswell Retardation Center in Mississippi.) It is summarized below.

When the issue of integration of individuals who are both elderly as well as diagnosed as mentally retarded is discussed, it is necessary that two areas be considered. These areas are both physical integration and psychosocial integration. The requirement to be met for physically integrating an elderly mentally retarded individual into a setting is the legal right to do so. M. M. possessed the adaptive living skills required for admission as well as the financial resources (supplemental security income) needed in order to live in this setting. The psychosocial integration of M. M. was facilitated by a number of factors. The first was that although he had a diagnostic history of being mentally retarded, he was mildly retarded intellectually and possessed the level of adaptive functioning which made it quite possible for him to "pass" as non-retarded within the particular setting in which he was placed. His affability was also quite an asset, for he was able to discuss many of the same topics as discussed by others, particularly men, who resided within that setting.

M. M. had retired from the vocational services available prior to his moving into the community, but was involved in both the Foster Grandparent and the Retired Senior Volunteer Program offered by the local aging service system. His involvement within these two organizations as an active member facilitated his involvement with his peers outside of the facility when he was moved into the community. Some of his fellow participants in both programs were residing in the same complex, as well as attending the local church and the local nutrition site.

The approach taken to integrate M. M. psychosocially into the local church and nutrition site was that of pairing him with a "friend" or "buddy." His particular "friend" was a person who knew M. M. from the mental retardation facility, had enjoyed his company within that setting, and who was more than happy to remain involved with him following his movement to the community. One other factor that facilitated his psychosocial integration was the fact that M. M. was viewed by others as interdependent rather than a dependent individual. M. M. never failed to attend a fellowship supper without bringing either a bowl of food or a package of rolls to be heated. He always participated in the other chores surrounding such an event, as did the other men. We felt it most important that he be viewed as a "contributor" to the event and not just a "receiver," with all the work being done by others.

In our network of services, the phrase "quality of life" is operationally defined as the options and choices one has in one's own life over "the day to day decisions which affect me."

M. M.'s situation clearly demonstrates the planning and thinking necessary for the success of his transition and integration into and acceptance by the general community. It shows how M. M. was helped to remain connected to his past activities of social functioning. It further indicates the continuity of interest and help by understanding professional care givers of the institutional staff at crucial points in M. M.'s life, which contributed greatly to his successful adaptions in the general community. This demonstrates that deinstitutionalization can work well when it is handled by knowledgeable, caring professionals who are given a clear focus for their functions and time to carry out those functions.

PROFESSIONAL FUNCTIONS OUTSIDE
JOB LIMITS

In this work the phrase "involvement of professionals" means that professional health care and/or social service providers go beyond the parameters of their usual job functions with regard to the chronically disabled elderly. These efforts may result in volunteer activities by the individual provider or in new responsibilities within the professional assignment when specific needs of the patient/client are perceived. Such interest and activities may influence the development of a different or new service by the institution or organization that then becomes institutionalized to meet the unmet needs of a number of clients.

When a new or enhanced service is planned by an agency or organization, often it is necessary to involve other organizations on a funding basis and/or other disciplines to support, supplement, complement, or complete the service in order to meet perceived needs. This melding of more than one organization and/or discipline is the core of interdisciplinary functioning which helps everyone involved to look at the patient/client in a more holistic fashion. The example below is this type of activity.

One of the outstanding needs of family care givers of Alzheimer's patients was found, through a statewide survey and from family support groups, to be respite care (McGinnis & Midura 1985: 43). Day care centers for Alzheimer patients helped, but they did not serve all those who were able to use them. Also, day care centers usually could not accommodate the more deteriorated person still living at home. Family support groups also made clear that previously available "sitters," when available and affordable, often did not know how to deal with the afflicted family member. All these factors led the staff of one Alzheimer's Association chapter to develop a "respite registry." This concept also was fueled by a grant obtained by the national Alzheimer's Association from the National Institute of Mental Health to "develop a program to initiate, and a national movement to provide respite services through the chapters" (*ADRDA Newsletter* 1984: 5). The respite registry now is an integral part of the chapter program.

The proposal to establish the respite registry was submitted to the NIMH Services Systems branch on March 20, 1986, and the contract was signed eleven months later. A staff line was developed for education and training in August 1987. The chapter staff with input from its administration, nurses, and social workers had drafted a comprehensive "assessment tool" to be used when families applied for either day care or respite care services. The same tool is used as a guide to match families with respite registry graduates (Draft of the assessment tool was presented at the Georgia Gerontology Society meeting, October 1987).

The material for this section came from a January 28, 1988, interview with the respite registry director and from internal documents made available. The director's first assignment was to publicize the program locally via speaking engagements plus notices in neighborhood papers. The first class started in May 1987 (Staff, April 1987, Atlanta Area Chapter Respite Registry to Begin. *ADRDA Newsletter:* 1).

The basic curriculum originally consisted of an Alzheimer's knowledge pretest; an overview of ADRDA, the respite registry, normal aging, and Alzheimer's disease; communicating with Alzheimer patients; role of the respite worker, medication, and potential side effects information; nutrition tips; ethics of care giving; personal care management; disaster preparedness; transfers and range of motion exercises; activities for persons with Alzheimer's; safety measures and infection control; record keeping; rescue breathing, airway obstruction, CPR; and three days of practicum in the AA day care center; plus a final quiz before graduation.

Upon successful graduation the respite workers are added to the registry for available work. They are certified for a six-month period. There is supervision by AA case managers, bimonthly meetings for discussion, and monthly in-service training for updating. Respite workers need to work a minimum of thirty-two hours per month and attend a minimum of three in-service sessions each six months to renew their certification.

The families requesting this service interview two or more referred workers (whenever possible) and hire one. They pay the chapter on a sliding scale. The AA pays full salary to the respite workers, subsidized, if necessary, by the NIMH and the Area Agency on Aging with Title III funds.

The registry started with a registered nurse, an MSW social worker, the director, and support staff. This interdisciplinary staff was very attentive and sensitive to the needs and problems expressed by their students. The director explained that the form and structure of the class was altered, if necessary, after each session and for each successive class in order to meet student needs. The educational backgrounds of the adjunct faculty varied, and the instructors focused on their own discipline, thereby covering the interdisciplinary needs of the Alzheimer patient.

The various modes of follow-up through in-service education, peer discussions, and ongoing supervision by case managers all help the respite workers stay involved with the agency and provide support against burnout on a stressful, lonely job. Pegging the hourly pay above the minimum wage, flexible hours, and recognition of the workers as a person all help prevent high rates of attrition. Use of experienced registry workers as role models, which has become part of the practicum for new workers, provides recognition and status which may be unique in health care settings. This service is affordable for most families, the respite workers make it accessible, and the combined efforts of the involved disciplines, the board, lay people from support groups, and government funding together make it available.

Many factors contributed to the success of this respite registry. First, the need for the service to be accessible, affordable, and available. Second, the determination of the staff to maintain a high quality of care similar to that found in their day care centers. Third, the staff's willingness to listen to the needs of the students and adjust the curriculum to meet their needs. A fourth factor is the certification and continuing in-service education using a variety of methods. In addition to upgrading skills, the group sessions help to counterbalance the professional isolation of working alone. A fifth factor is that pay for the workers is above minimum wage and graded to the complexity of care necessary, as well as to recognition and status for experience.

The interdisciplinary focus came from the chapter's staff, emphasizing that service and care can be comprehensive and holistic only when all the necessary disciplines function cooperatively toward that goal.

Involvement of professionals with an elderly mentally retarded individual in the community was outlined in the previous section, where they contributed to the social functioning and quality of life of that individual. In M. M.'s situation, his successful deinstitutionalization was planned and followed up by the retardation center's multidisciplinary staff with the help of volunteers and community agencies.

The process of mainstreaming mentally retarded elderly into senior centers requires extending the functions of involved professionals and the involvement of various disciplines and organizations. As explained by Dr. Cotten (personal written communication to the author, June 1988), the following factors need to be met:

1. The administration of the community senior center needs to be willing to provide the potential participant with the opportunity for such an experience. The appropriate staff at the center needs to be involved in the selection of the persons to attend.

2. The mental retardation network needs to evaluate the potential recipient for this experience, which may differ from the annual interdisciplinary evaluation provided to each client.

3. The senior center staff needs to have criteria for admission to its program. This is reviewed by the interdisciplinary team of the retardation center, which then recommends specific individuals.

4. The senior center staff and the interdisciplinary team meet to review the recommendations, then interact with the clients. Those clients mutually agreed upon then attend the center on a probationary basis.

5. Those people unable to integrate even after training opportunities are removed from the program but are available for services to the "frail elderly."

6. Continual "cross-training" of staffs in the mental retardation network and the aging network (senior center) is imperative. This includes opportunities for involvement of representatives of both networks in professional meetings and conferences, as well as in presentations to both staffs on an in-service or local basis. Both network staffs need to be committed to cooperation and communication.

7. The provision of case management services for elderly mentally retarded individuals plus all the other interactions make it possible to establish an affiliation with the staff of the cen-

ter, the Area Agency on Aging, other city agencies, and the local university. Because of these affiliations, potential problems can be addressed, thus reducing the likelihood of limiting options and choices. In this way a better quality of life for elderly mentally retarded people can be provided.

This summation has been included because it indicates the following: the interdisciplinary nature and complexity of developing new services for hitherto unserved populations; the persistence over time needed to establish a new service; and the involvement and commitment of both administrative and program levels of staff, as well as the involvement of other public and private organizations. The initial planning, organization, and actual development of a new cooperative program requires much administrative and program staff time which may seem, to boards of directors, funding bodies, or others, out of proportion to the numbers who will benefit. However, once the basic groundwork, methods and procedures, and goals have been put in place, enhanced services for many more people becomes possible.

ORGANIZATION OR INSTITUTION INVOLVEMENT

Organizations frequently develop from an unmet need perceived by a group of people who may start out as a self-help or support group; by professionals concerned about a particular disease entity; or by an educational body. Sometimes they start as demonstration programs. Goals, characteristics, and major functions of national organizations concerned with a health problem generally include development of local chapters, education about the problem with both local and national publicity, education of appropriate governmental bodies, local and national fund-raising, some provision of services to patients and their families, and funding research on causative factors, techniques, and methods to alleviate and/or cure the problem (this is abstracted from the annual reports of a number of national health organizations).

The focus of the organization may change over the years as some goals are met. Usually these organizations are nonprofit and national in scope and become known to the general public through media publicity and sponsorship by well-known personalities.

The examples in this section will start with the smaller one related to mental retardation. It covered three geographic areas in one state and involved twenty-five different service agencies. It can be categorized more properly as a time-limited consortium of organizations united to provide needed services to a heretofore "neglected" population. Because of its common goal, it is used as an example of an organization here, although its philosophy, purposes, and functions are more specific than those generalized above.

The Mississippi Elderly Developmentally Disabled Persons Project was a demonstration project funded by the Mississippi Developmental Disabilities Program through the Bureau of Mental Retardation, Mississippi Department of Mental Health, and administered by the Boswell Retardation Center, an agency of the Mississippi Department of Mental Health. The undergirding philosophy of this project emanated from a realization that elderly developmentally disabled (DD) persons comprise a diverse population

> representing various intellectual, adaptive and medical levels. The purpose of the Project is to plan and implement a cost-effective service delivery system, based upon comprehensive functional assessments, that is community based and is designed to identify and meet the needs of elderly developmentally disabled individuals residing in two urban and one rural area. . . . A case management approach is utilized to access services for clients . . . enabling the case manager and client to explore options together. . . . Another key component of the project is inter-agency cooperation. Project clients are served by a variety of living arrangements, day programs and support services. (From the brochure "They Grow Old Too," Mississippi Elderly Developmentally Disabled Persons Project, n.d.)

The Final Narrative Report presented to the Bureau of Mental Retardation, Mississippi Department of Mental Health, October 16, 1987, provides more specifics. It is summarized below:

> A survey of all available resources was conducted in the target areas. Aging and mental retardation staffs were educated of [sic] the special needs of elderly DD persons. Case management service plans were developed for each client by appropriate Center and Project staff. Wherever possible, families of clients

also were involved. The needs addressed included alternative living arrangements, mental health care, day programming, speech therapy, medical care, and others.

Demographically, the clients all were residing in the community; none were on waiting lists for state residential facilities, and none were returned to the community from state residential facilities. However, 10 are at high risk of entering more restrictive environments if Project funds are discontinued.

A major common need for the retired clients (76% of all Project clients) was day programming or enhanced opportunities/activities at available Senior Centers. Nutrition sites were available to most clients. Referrals were made to 25 different services during 1987. These included 6 clients referred to a variety of residential settings, 2 clients referred to nutrition sites, 12 clients referred to Senior Centers, 9 clients referred to specialized day programs, 9 referred to needed transportation services, 5 referred to the county Human Resource Agency, 21 referred to AARP, and 10 clients needed referral to a variety of medical care resources.

Other organizations and agencies, not the Project itself, furnished the transportation services, senior centers, mental health, health and dental services and nutrition services, as well as work and adult activity center opportunities. All these were used regularly. The service delivery systems for the Project clients was planned to encompass services from aging, mental health/mental retardation and generic resources. New services were developed only where gaps occurred.

The major problems in implementing the program related to prejudices and attitudes of those in the aging and generic service systems restricting the elderly mentally retarded from participating with other elderly. This problem was overcome by planful [sic] and careful "cross-training" of the staffs of the services systems and the careful comprehensive functional assessments of clients before introducing them to the general community services.

The major accomplishments of the Project have been an effective and appropriate delivery system for elderly DD in the general community. Also, "keen insights into this population's special needs and capabilities were acquired," and "cross-training" of aging, generic and mental health/mental retardation staffs occurred. The report makes a very strong plea for continuation of funds for the Project. (Cotton & Wentworth 1987: 1–6 passim)

This is an example of public funding working through a public agency, the Boswell Retardation Center, which coordinated services and education among public and private agencies. The brief overview given very clearly indicates the interrelationship and complexity of health and social services, which must function cooperatively and in collaboration if elderly chronically disabled are to function at their fullest.

A basic question raised by this project, which also occurs with many demonstration projects, is funding for its continuation. When programs demonstrate their effectiveness in service provision and cost effectiveness vis-à-vis alternative solutions, what happens when funding, which is time-limited, comes to an end? Is it possible and feasible to seek other funding? Many private foundations are reluctant to fund the ongoing costs of worthwhile programs. Government sources also are reluctant, particularly during this period, to add new programs of service, no matter how much they are needed. The clients in this project and their families were hardly in a position to provide major financial help.

Is it possible and feasible for United Way campaigns to include this type of project, instead of funding only established programs and institutions on an ongoing basis? Could communal and fraternal organizations adopt such projects by providing some funds and volunteers toward their continuance? Is it possible to interest adjunct—that is, family members or "alumni" of service providers—to help with funding and volunteers? If, early in its development, the project had organized a community board of directors, could they have organized advocacy efforts and fund-raising drives to continue it? Would national religious groups allot some funds for such projects? Would large businesses, especially those employing the DD, support such projects? These questions indicate the complexity and innovative thinking necessary to continue effective time-limited demonstration projects.

The Alzheimer's Association is a comparatively young national organization. It began with the efforts, over a period of nine years, of

Jerome H. Stone to find some answers, some relief, and some help for his wife's condition, which was thought to be presenile dementia by the physicians he consulted (Stone 1982: 39–40). Stone read all he could find about Alzheimer's disease, then "I haunted the major medical centers for help." He did discover that a few centers were doing some research on Alzheimer's disease. The Albert Einstein School of Medicine suggested he contact its chief of Neurology, who was involved with a family support group.

> In October 1979 the National Institute on Health called a meeting to explore the possibility of a national organization on Alzheimer's disease. The Directors of the National Institute on Aging, and of the National Institute of Neurological and Communicative Disorders had found seven family support groups in the United States concerned with this problem. Representatives of these groups and Mr. J. Stone were invited to this meeting with top educators in the field. All felt a national organization would help those dealing with Alzheimer's both personally and professionally. From this small group Stone and others worked to organize a national organization, utilizing his business career and organizational experience to mold its development. The name chosen was Alzheimer's Disease and Related Disorders Association (ADRDA). [In 1988, it was changed to the Alzheimer's Association.] Stone called on experts in the self-help field to help structure and focus the new group. In addition to Board Members from the original family support groups, it was agreed to have "Public Board Members" responsible only to the national organization. "Dear Abby" provided the name and address of the new organization. Subsequently, the office received 25,000 pieces of mail with inquiries! Those names, plus those from the original seven chapters became the basic mailing list.
>
> By 1982, the influence of ADRDA included a mailing list of 80,000 names, 58 chapters with 250 support groups. The Board grew from 10 to 44 members. The Medical and Scientific Advisory Board was added with 24 leaders in medicine and education. Also, in 1982, the first research fund provided seven grants awarded under the guidance of the Medical and Scientific Advisory Board. A quarterly national newspaper had been started for members, and the public media had been provided

with educational material which was publicized widely on radio,
T.V. and in newspapers. (Stone 1982: 39–40)

The Alzheimer's Association did not depend only on a ground swell
from the public to influence national activity. Stone saw the need for
treatment, respite care, and other ancillary services, but if these were
to be available on a national basis, there needed to be federal involvement. Therefore, the AA retained CR Associates, a consulting firm
in Washington, D.C., to advise it on governmental relations. First,
the consulting firm devised a strategy on education ". . . focused primarily on those officials who were in the best positions to effect
changes in government policy" (Ruscio & Cavarocci 1984: 12–15). At
the same time the AA board members and executive committee met
with members of congressional committees with jurisdiction over
medical research, long-term care, and federal appropriations.

The next big task was to develop a document that "would give
federal policymakers a broader view of the problem and a better
sense of the frustrations experienced by families seeking help from
their government" (12–15). The AA applied itself to this task after
extensive discussions with physicians, scientists, and family members
and formulated its "National Plan to Conquer Alzheimer's Disease."
The document addressed the broad issues of medical research, long-
term care, family support services, disability benefits, and veteran's
care. The document subsequently was reprinted in its entirety in the
Congressional Record.

The national AA office promotes public awareness, maintains liai-
sons with government agencies and national professional organizations, stimulates family support activities, administers a research grant
program, serves as a clearinghouse for information, and publishes a
quarterly newsletter.

The meteoric rise of this organization was due to many factors,
among which were the drive and determination of its founders, the
desperate need for help and support for family care givers, the meaningful involvement of the Medical and Scientific Advisory Board to
provide consultation and expertise, the inclusion of business leaders
on the board and celebrity figures to help with fund-raising, the hiring
of professional consultants to guide the Association in its dealing with
federal governmental bodies, and its focused contact with federal officials and committees. Yet another factor that helped the AA start

on a solid basis was the presence of knowledgeable people from a variety of professional disciplines—physicians, nurses, social workers, lawyers, to name a few—along with family care-giving members on its board, all interacting and learning from each other. Funds to enable the national organization to function in many spheres did not appear to be a problem, even at the beginning.

The organizational format, in essence, leaves the chapters free to focus on those issues pertinent to the local situation, while they are connected to the national body through dues, publicity of special programs, awards, and so on. The national newsletter, in addition to articles about national programs, research, and various chapter activities, usually has one article that is directly helpful to the care giver. This formula seems to have worked very well.

There are a few major questions to be raised. What is the extent of coordination and clearance among grants allotted by the federal government, the AA, and other private foundations for research on Alzheimer's disease? Is there duplication of effort and money to discover the same material? Have other equally devastating chronic problems, such as AIDS, not received the attention, investigation, effort, and money needed? Would it be more helpful to people with chronic devastating diseases if the federal government was pushed to war on all of these?

GOVERNMENT INVOLVEMENT

Federal government programs, service, and support for older people who have chronic disabilities is very complex, spanning many agencies and institutions. The federal government provides both direct financial help, through Social Security, Medicare, Supplementary Security Income (SSI), and Medicaid to eligible individuals, and indirect help through grants to governmental and nongovernmental organizations. Medicare is direct federal help which is automatic for those who reach age sixty-five. Medicaid and SSI are means tested for the very poor and disabled of all ages. Federal funds also provide many other needed services at the federal, regional, and state levels. Some examples are congregate nutrition sites, senior centers, multipurpose senior centers, community mental health centers, senior citizen public housing, and transportation for the elderly and disabled. Rich and Baum (1984: 11–12) point out that thirteen committees of the House of Representatives have jurisdiction over eighteen program areas serving elderly people and that eleven committees of the Senate have jurisdiction over eighteen program areas. They continue:

> Officers of the Administration on Aging (AoA) were responsible for regulating and monitoring activities carried out under the Older Americans Act (OAA). The AoA administrative control goes through 10 regional offices, each responsible for a cluster of states. Each regional office oversees the state Unit on Aging, which is responsible for activities on behalf of older Americans. State Units on Aging oversee the Area Agencies on Aging (AAA) which represent regional divisions within each state. The AAAs contract out to local nonprofit service programs most of the direct services mandated under the OAA. (48–49)

The OAA also administers discretionary funds as grants for demonstration, education, research, and training related to older people. For the fiscal year 1987, there were 264 grants active during October, allotted primarily to colleges and universities, with a substantial minority to state agencies and a sprinkling to private organizations (AoA Grant Compendium, FY 1987, Jan 1, 1988). Perusal of that year's compendium indicated that nineteen, or less than 1 percent of the total number of grants, focused directly on the disabilities studied in this book. Most seemed focused primarily on education and training of educators, professionals, and paraprofessionals; only one seemed devoted primarily to research.

Other federal agencies providing grants relating to aging include four divisions of the National Institutes of Health, the Veterans Administration, the Health Resources and Services Administration under the Department of Health and Human Services, the Administration on Developmental Disabilities, and the Public Health Office of Disease Prevention and Health Promotion.

The Atlanta Area Chapter of the AA submitted a proposal to the governor subsequent to 1984 amendments to the OAA, who referred it to the Georgia Department of Human Resources (DHR) to develop a statewide task force to explore how the public and private sectors could assist Alzheimer's disease victims and their family care givers. The commissioner of the DHR delegated the responsibility for conducting this study to the (Georgia) State Office of Aging. All material following is summarized from the report of the Study Committee (McGinnis & Midura 1985: 6, 25–26, 37, 39, 41–53).

Co-chairmen of the Study Committee were the Director of the Office of Aging and the Advocacy Chairman of the Atlanta Area Chapter of the AA. It was a broad-based committee which included legislators, representatives from appropriate departments within state government and from appropriate health planning and service agencies, health educators, academicians, and public and private gerontology experts. The Study Committee on Alzheimer's disease was formed in July 1985 and completed its assignments by that December. The mandate was to examine the nature and extent of Alzheimer's disease and related disorders in Georgia, identify available resources and gaps in needed services, and develop policy recommendations. The policy recommendations covered improved patient care and services, increased public awareness of this problem, financial assistance and social supports to patients and family members, further research, and better coordination of state activities and legislative initiatives.

The Study Committee used four subcommittees to carry out its responsibilities: Data and Demography, Resources and Services, Training and Education, and Finances and Funding.

The subcommittees carried out their work through a vigorous review of the literature and extant research including federal and state reports; through consultation with local and nationally recognized experts; through five different questionnaires or survey instruments which were developed and mailed to over 2,500 service providers and care givers; and through four community forums, with over four hundred attendees, which were held around the state to hear testimony from local service providers and family care givers. Additionally, committee members participated in training sessions, legislative committee meetings, and in a variety of public education and public media information and education interviews. The social, psychological, and physical drain on the family care givers was captured in testimony received at the public hearings and is summarized in the final report, which includes all the recommendations of the four subcommittees.

Some of the financial recommendations included: tax credits for care givers, encouragement of long-term care health insurance, inclusion of Alzheimer and other dementia patients in all public definitions of disability, adjustment of Medicaid reimbursement policies to include AD patients, and raise rates of respite care payments to be comparable to other in-home services.

Some of the direct service recommendations included establishing more day care and respite services, expanding the Community Care program [a Medicaid waiver program providing services to support frail elderly at home who are at risk of institutionalization]; permitting Medicaid to allow care givers to retain sufficient funds to maintain themselves; expanding the Alzheimer's Community Support Project of the DHR to include training about AD to direct patient care staffs of hospitals, nursing homes, and home health care agencies; developing short-term out-of-home respite programs by nursing homes, hospitals and other groups; and establishing regional diagnostic and treatment centers.

The education committee recommended that the State Office of Aging develop, with the various AAAs, local inventories of available services and resources; widely distribute *The Senior Citizens Handbook: Laws and Programs Affecting Senior Citizens in Georgia;* provide public education about long-term care insurance policies and benefits available in the state; stimulate evaluation of the existing nursing home Patient Bill of Rights and other appropriate documents to make them more responsive to the needs of dementia patients; and stimulate other appropriate public agencies to enforce the Disabled Adults Protection Act and Patient Bill of Rights more stringently.

Education recommendations for health care organizations and institutions included encouraging appropriate organizations to provide continuing education to physicians on the diagnosis, care, and treatment of patients with dementias, and if appropriate, recommend inclusion of curriculum in medical schools about AD and related disorders; checking licensing board exams of physicians, nurses, and allied health professions for inclusion of material on AD and other dementias; and encouraging both public and private organizations to urge the medical community, state agencies, and academic institutions to apply for federal money related to Alzheimer's research.

It was further recommended that the State Office of Aging should function as a clearinghouse to update a statewide data base of individuals with AD and related disorders annually; research statutes and regulations concerning definitions of disability to ensure such patients are not precluded from benefits due others; collect, analyze, and dis-

seminate information on federal grants; coordinate efforts among educational institutions; make recommendations to the legislative
Long-Term Care Insurance Study Committee; and offer its assistance
in the assessment of proposed insurance policies.

The State Office of Aging should appoint a committee to advocate, coordinate, and ensure the implementation of the study committee's recommendations, which would provide an annual report on progress
toward the goals. All parent organizations of members of this committee
should support and advocate for all recommendations contained in the
final report. The members of the General Assembly on the Study Committee should introduce a resolution in the General Assembly recogniz-
ing the extent of Alzheimer's disease and related disorders in Georgia;
the efforts of the Alzheimer's Disease Study Committee; and the Study
Committee's report and final recommendations.

Most of the recommendations were couched positively and carefully. The only times the word "advocate" was used in the report was
in relation to the Office of Aging for follow-up activities and to members of the Study Committee to support and advocate the recommendations within their own organizations. Although it is difficult to
find in the final report the authority, or clout, needed to implement
recommendations, the variety of interests among the Study Committee members tended to ensure support and cooperation for its recommendations when necessary. The full report and recommendations
were approximately 95 percent implemented in a cooperative, coordinated fashion by the Study Committee members. Many recommendations were incorporated into subsequent appropriate state
regulations and standards. This example clearly indicates that those
involved with a disability can affect the legislative process, policy development, and government decision making. Longitudinal follow-up
is necessary to determine just how effective this excellent first step
was.

Another study involving the aging network and the developmentally
disabled (DD) network is too complex to be included as an example
here. Only the most innovative of the major findings and recommendations applicable to other states are summarized below (Rose &
Ansello 1987: 50–77):

There is a need to develop information about services to the many
DD over age sixty who are unknown to the DD network, provider
agencies, and advocacy groups. There is a need to clarify which agen-

cies are responsible to serve the older DD/MR population, the locus of services, and their implementation. Public officials and others who develop policies need more information on DD and aging to develop viable policy initiatives to change existing federal and state regulations, which impede the provision of age-appropriate programs and services for older people with DD/MR.

Agencies need to be innovative to coordinate programs and services and develop joint funding mechanisms to maximize existing programs to ensure an appropriate range of services.

There needs to be recognition that administrators and program personnel often have difficulty stepping out of their historical identities. There are many concerned public and private organizations and agencies in both service networks which are not always aware of what the others are doing.

It is suggested that the aging network serve DD persons who are appropriate and the DD network serve those with late-life disabilities such as dementia. Formerly normal elders, who now are frail and disoriented, can profit from the DD system of day programs where the staff is more attuned to dealing with such behavior and where the staff ratio is more helpful to them.

The Job Partnership and Training Act and the Older Americans Act can be oriented to provide training for DD/MR persons to become companions for the old-old frail elders, and for healthy elders to serve as companions to DD elders. They suggest that some funds from the DD system could follow their clients into the aging system. [This author adds that the reverse also might be appropriate if aging system clients enter the DD system.]

The need for cross-training in both the DD and aging systems is stressed for educators and staffs at all levels from high school through professional school and from direct service providers to state directors of departments. Staff and student internship exchanges in health care and social service disciplines might be very helpful for greater exposure to the operations of complementary service systems.

Rose and Ansello (1987) learned that there is tremendous interest in learning more about the intersections of aging and DD by families, legislators and government officials, managers, and service providers. These authors suggest it is better to explore the use of each other's expertise and resources instead of creating special subsystems:

"Changes or innovations should begin at both the top and the bottom organizationally. . . . "

The authors also found that similar functional abilities of both groups of elderly suggest similar services, and that differences call for more supervision and supports.

Planning and establishing a system of comprehensive services for DD and MR elders requires the development of strong linkages among all the resources needed by these people, which already exist within both the aging and DD/MR systems.

Rose and Ansello also point out that most of the current DD programs are geared to active treatment of a primarily younger age group. With older DD/MR clients there is a need to shift the emphasis toward prevention of regression or preservation of skills. In addition realistic goals need to be set for these persons with the same options for service as for the nondisabled person in pursuit of personal growth and development.

The report concludes with a focus on education and training, which had been emphasized throughout.

The findings in this report clearly relate to Illsley's (1981) term "dependency groups," as well as to the "cross-training" emphasized by Cotten and Wentworth (1987). Rose and Ansello continuously stress the need for the aging and DD/MR networks to take appropriate responsibility so that their clients can receive the most appropriate comprehensive care and services in the least restrictive and cost effective way. This author again wants to emphasize that the health and social services industries, both public and private, need to coordinate their services to the disabled.

The statewide Alzheimer's study was conducted by a state agency, the Office of Aging, using an interdisciplinary committee of volunteers who focused primarily on one chronic problem. Its policy recommendations included actions needed to be taken by the state legislature; many have already been implemented. The "Research and Planning Study on Aging and Developmental Disabilities," conducted by a state university, was federally funded. Its findings and recommendations focus more on training, education, and collaboration in the two service systems and for amendments to national legislation. Both types of study and recommendations are necessary for appropriate comprehensive services to be provided in the least restrictive setting and least costly manner.

HEALTH INSURANCE: LONG-TERM CARE

No work about older people and their disabilities which attempts to be comprehensive can omit the financing of health care and role of health insurance. This section deals with long-term care insurance where, fortunately, there is an example available. Medicare and Medicaid are covered in the next chapter, health maintenance organizations in chapter 4. Aspects of all forms of health insurance germane to the disability under discussion will be noted appropriately.

Long-term care of the elderly disabled has been addressed in a fragmented manner in the past, largely as a biomedical enterprise. Long-term care seems to have eluded any significant solution for many reasons, including the fact that until relatively recently "a comprehensive solution to long-term care has not been sought" (Estes & Lee 1985: 17). The Pepper Commission Report as well as others have begun to address this situation.

Four special characteristics of long-term care are noted by Rivlin and Wiener (1988: 13–15):

1. Only a minority of the elderly have large long-term care or nursing home care expenses.

2. If people wait until retirement age to begin buying insurance or accumulating assets to pay for care, the premium payments or level of savings required is large.

3. The rising cost of long-term care presents special problems. The price of nursing home and home care is likely to rise faster than general inflation which magnifies the financial risks for both the users of and those who supply insurance.

4. Because such a large percentage of long-term care services now are performed voluntarily by relatives, the use of paid services may increase significantly once third-party financing is available, especially as the number of disabled and elderly increases.

Many people who could medically qualify for paid services are not receiving any due to their lack of funds. On balance the increase in nursing home use induced by expanded availability of third-party payments is likely to be modest. In the case of home care services, the increase in use is likely to be substantial (*Changing Times,* September 1986: 9).

Concern about long-term health care blossomed publicly during the 1980s (Roemer 1982: 122–124; Harrington et al., 1985: 42–88; Califano [by implication] 1986: 210–212; Ginzberg 1988: 3647–3649; Rivlin & Wiener 1988: 13–15). At a forum on long-term health care at the Carter Center in 1989, material distributed included reprints of articles in newspapers and popular magazines from across the country. Six appeared in 1987 and thirteen in 1988.

The big private insurance companies also have begun to explore long-term care. *Consumer Reports* (May 1988: 300–302) found seventy companies offering long-term care insurance. These companies had a wide variety of eligibility requirements, types of benefits offered, costs to policy holders, limitations on benefits, exclusion of preexisting conditions, and length of time benefits apply. Each company provided its own definition of each variable. The report evaluated fifty-three policies and found twelve excluded coverage for home health care. The same article also found "virtually all the policies exclude care for mental and nervous disorders." About half of the policies had statements such as "we won't pay for confinements due to mental illnesses except those with demonstrable organic disease." No policy paid for stays in rest homes, old age homes, mental hospitals, or alcohol and drug rehabilitation centers.

The home care benefits in long-term insurance are of particular interest because many chronic disabilities require them on an ongoing or intermittent basis. Some companies include this as a separate policy or as a rider at an additional premium. A few include adult day care center and hospice care also as a separate policy or rider at an additional premium. Some policies require previous nursing home or hospital confinement and start paying for home care if it starts within fourteen days after such confinement. Generally policies without such limitations begin payment as soon as "the regular waiting period" ends. "Policies usually pay home-care benefits until the regular benefit period maximum has run out," but this can vary from thirty days to three years. The *Consumer Reports* evaluation was the most complete one found at that time.

The example for this section is part of the report of the statewide committee on Alzheimer's disease, used earlier, that led to efforts to influence state legislation about long-term care insurance.

The subcommittee on finance and funding consisted of a state representative, a designee of a state senator, an advocacy chairman, a care giver from the local chapter of the AA, an attorney with the Legal Services Program, and staff from the Office of Aging. From July to December 1985 they reviewed all available material on long-term care insurance (McGinnis & Midura, The Alzheimer's Study Committee Report, 1985: 37).

The financing subcommittee received material from the senior policy analyst in the Senate Research Office (Lee 1985) which was prepared for the Long-Term Care Insurance Study Committee of the Senate. The Senate Research Office material (used with D. V. Lee's permission) included an analysis by the Michigan Insurance Bureau of the responsibilities and authorities of major elements of the health care system and a graphic analysis of the interactions and conflicts among principal components in the Michigan health care system (no date was provided). The latter clearly showed the stresses and contradictory goals among consumers, providers, third party payers, and regulatory bodies. Other material included information on the experience of the Fireman's Fund of the American Life Insurance Company by Robert F. Phillips and a long-term care insurer's perspective by Arthur Lifson of the Equitable Life Assurance Society of the United States. (No date or name was given for these articles, except that the material was compiled by the American Health Care Association.)

In addition to all this material, the senior policy analyst "provided a brief description of problems associated with the growing demand for long-term care when coupled with the general unavailability [in 1985] of this form of insurance coverage" (Lee 1985). Lee first documents the need for and cost of long-term care insurance both federally and statewide. He then lists and explains the major reasons for the lack of sufficient private insurance:

- Difficulties in assessing the demand for long-term care coverage and marketing strategies; including competition with public coverage leading to private under-utilization.
- Premium pricing difficulties related to inflation and what is customary and usual.
- State and federal regulatory restrictions including state variations relating long-term care to medigap policies.

- Definitional inconsistencies as to skilled, intermediate, and custodial long-term care.

- Lack of group marketing plans which broaden the base of risk when purchased by employers.

- The possibility of insurance-induced demand which might lead to overutilization if nursing home care is reimbursed. (Lee 1985)

Granted that the list and explanations were tightly condensed for the purposes of Lee's memorandum. They nevertheless follow the medical model: equating long-term care with nursing home admissions. The senior policy analyst did not mention any kind of outpatient services, community support services, or help for family care givers. He also invited the finance subcommittee to a meeting of the senate long-term care insurance study committee, at which the insurance industry in the State would respond to the long-term care problem.

The finance subcommittee made its report after consulting with authorities on federal and state programs, carefully reviewing the literature, examining relevant legislation from other states in depth, and analyzing results of questionnaires, surveys, and testimony from the public forums. It decided to "concentrate on those issues and state programs which lend themselves more easily to immediate impact and changes and avoid the long-range changes in national policies." The members of the subcommittee felt their recommendations, in the main, could be accomplished with existing resources after some realignment of priorities. They then listed recommendations for quality care and definitions and legalities for Alzheimer patients (McGinnis & Midura 1985: 37).

Most of their recommendations were made to the state senate committee on long-term care insurance. They urged the committee to encourage the development of long-term care insurance capabilities. Beyond that, the subcommittee stressed the importance of such insurance to assist AD patients and their families, to focus on functional abilities of patients, to include both physical and mental impairments, and to provide both in-home and community-based supports as well as institutional care. Their other recommendations offered help of the local AA chapter and the Office of Aging to the insurance commissioner in reviewing proposed policies to determine their potential impact and effectiveness.

Community education needs to be widespread to make the general public aware of the need for long-term care insurance and develop the skill to evaluate policies for potential benefits. "Care must be taken to strike a balance between regulation and the need for an informed consumer population" (McGinnis & Midura 1985: 39).

An interesting contrast to the Alzheimer's study committee report issued in December 1985 is the report of the Senate private long-term care insurance study committee issued at the same time (McKenzie 1985: 1–8). Its recommendations appear to focus on nurturing the development of private long-term care insurance in the state with general oversight by the office of the insurance commissioner and appropriate legislative bodies. It ended its interim report by stating that "the committee has established a special interest in seeing that private long-term-care insurance policies are developed, and it will remain committed to monitoring this development as well as ensuring that these policies are marketed in a fair manner" (3–6).

It is obvious that the Alzheimer's study committee, with its emphasis on the effects of chronic disability on persons and families, focused on comprehensive long-term health care needs, whereas the senate committee focused on nurturing and encouraging nursing home insurance policies. The only standards the Senate committee seemed interested in at that time were those that applied to marketing and selling policies, with barely a mention of appropriate care. The thrust was to encourage all insurance companies to sell in this state and attempt to set standards of care later.

In December 1985 the full report of the Alzheimer's Study Committee was presented to the General Assembly with all the recommendations from the four subcommittees. Subsequently many of the recommendations made by the Office of Aging and advocates from this Committee were incorporated into the long-term care insurance regulations adopted in Georgia, including the mandated coverage of Alzheimer's disease in all such policies as well as other consumer protections.

As a postscript to these 1985 efforts, note the following developments: Early in 1987 the Office of Aging issued a guide for buying long-term care insurance. In October 1987 the Office of the Commissioner of Insurance issued a listing of companies with nursing home policies approved (thirty-three). The list is updated periodically, always with the qualifier "this list may not be complete." The state legislature submitted a bill of regulations for long-term care insurance which was signed and became law on July 1, 1988. The regulations were very explicit about the inclusion of Alzheimer's disease and other organic brain disorders, marketing with high integrity and clear clarification, the inclusion of all three levels of nursing home care and home health care, and provisions for spouses. By March 1989 regulations were adopted for long-term care insurance with many benefits to the public (Goldman 1989: 2). In 1990 the Long-Term Care Co-alition was formed, whose comprehensive guide for purchasing this type of insurance analyzed all policies approved for sale in this state and contained accurate information on premium costs.

This example shows that those with chronic disabilities and their care givers are able to influence the government to support their concerns and needs. The local chapter of the AA influenced the state Department of Human Resources to set up, through the Office of Aging, the statewide study committee on Alzheimer's disease. The inclusion of state elected representatives, appropriate public and private sector members, and a variety of health care professionals ensured a broad base of interest, support, and advocacy. The recommendations of this Committee had an impact on the senate committee on private long-term care insurance and also impacted the state insurance department, which resulted in a bill being signed into law. This law included a number of provisions related to a more comprehensive approach to long-term care than had been originally considered by the senate committee.

CHAPTER 3

Hearing Disability

A very common impairment of older people is loss of hearing, which can lead to disability. The best estimates in the United States indicate 368.0 men per 1,000 and 286.5 women per 1,000 over age 65 have this problem (Adams & Benson 1992: 84).

There are three general causes of hearing loss in the elderly: conductive, sensorineural, and central auditory disorders. Conductive disorders, which occur in the outer or middle ear, generally can be medically or surgically treated. The causes of this type of hearing loss can be earwax impacted in the outer ear canal (common in the aging ear), holes in the eardrum, fluid inside the middle ear, or interference with the movement of the middle ear bones. Sensorineural disorders affect the inner ear or auditory nerve. Causes of this can be loss of hair cells in the inner ear (from constant exposure to loud noises or aging) and tumors on the auditory nerve. Central auditory disorders result from problems within the brain. Usually both sensorineural and central auditory disorders cannot be treated medically or surgically (Williams, 1987: 2).

A disease specific to the aging body, presbycusis, is a communication disorder characterized by progressive degeneration of auditory function. This type of deterioration may mean

the simple loss of hearing sensitivity through chemical and mechanical changes in the inner ear and breakdown of the inner ear structures. More often, however, it refers to the complex degenerative changes occurring along the nerve pathways leading to the brain ... [which] may result in a slowing down of the signals traveling from the ear to the brain. (Williams 1987: 3)

The chronological age at which this process begins, as well as when the other ear disorders occur, varies with each individual, just as do the other aging processes. However, presbycusis does not affect everyone who ages. Environmental noise, certain drugs, improper diet, and genetic makeup may contribute to this disorder (National Institute on Aging 1983: 2).

Other problems related to the ear and hearing loss are tinnitus and Ménière's disease. Tinnitus is "the perception of sound in the absence of an acoustic stimulation ... a subjective experience ... [which] may be of a buzzing, ringing, roaring, whistling, or hissing quality ... that varies over time. [It] ... may be intermittent or continuous. An associated hearing loss is usually present" (Berkow 1982: 1082). The possible causes "remain obscure," and there is no known specific therapy at the present time. Treatment should be directed to the underlying disease, which may ameliorate tinnitus (1082).

Ménière's disease is "a disorder characterized by recurring prostrating vertigo, sensorineural hearing loss, and tinnitus associated with generalized dilation of the membranous labyrinth" (1086–1087). In recent years a difficult surgical procedure, retrolabyrinthine vestibular neurectomy, has been developed to relieve the disorder. Excessive fluid is drained, thus relieving pressure on the inner ear with little chance of hearing loss (Stern 1987: 12). Estimates from the National Health Interview Survey include hearing impairment and tinnitus but not Ménière's disease as a separate entity.

One important factor that contributes to hearing loss becoming a disability is that it is invisible to others (unless an assisting device is visible). The lack of awareness of the hearing loss by others can lead to impatience, frustration, irritation, and anger by both the one with the hearing loss and those who do hear.

Hearing loss in the elderly is not necessarily total deafness. It can take the form of reducing the loudness of sounds, distorting or blurring sounds, or recruitment, which is an abnormal growth in the loudness of a sound. The latter narrows the range between when a sound

is loud enough to hear and when it becomes too loud and painful
(Williams 1987: 1).

EFFECTS ON THE INDIVIDUAL

Any degree of hearing loss creates an alteration of the environment
for the affected person and the involved family. It has been pointed
out by Wax and DiPietro (1987: 2) that hearing occurs on three levels
of consciousness. The basic, or primitive, level is one of the ways we
keep in touch with the environment. For example, the singing of birds
and sounds of children playing help us feel connected and enhances
the quality of life. Signal or warning sounds such as police whistles,
sirens, automobile horns, the ping or buzz of electrical devices, door
bells, and telephone rings, when not heard, may cause problems of
safety or misfortune both inside and outside the home. The social, or
symbolic, level of hearing loss tends to lead to withdrawal and social
isolation when speech cannot readily be received and/or understood.
Other sounds that enhance the quality of life, such as music, drama,
movies, religious services, lectures, and discussions, also are no longer
available to those who are hearing impaired (mild hearing disorder)
or have hearing loss (profound impairment).

Once the person with hearing loss acknowledges this loss and begins to adapt to it, a number of strategies to maintain contact with
the hearing world can be used. Some of these coping strategies include pretending to understand, being alert to situational clues understood primarily through visual alertness, prior agreement with
hearing companions, acknowledging the disability openly, and requesting appropriate help (Wax & DiPietro 1987: 2–3).

There are a variety of aids and methods now available to help the
person with hearing loss. The first is a thorough physical examination,
including a sight and hearing evaluation. Then, if necessary, evaluation by an otologist or audiologist. Numerous devices now are available, including warning lights and signals instead of sounds on many
home appliances, telephones with a visual ring signaler and amplification, and the telecommunication device for deaf persons (TDD)
telephones.

American Sign Language forms a linguistic network community for
those who have learned this method of communication. Generally,
this applies to the developmentally hearing disabled. Mature people

have a history of hearing and speech, so they arrive at hearing problems with very different life experiences and histories than do young people. Learning to sign is not a prime goal for them. Preserving and utilizing all residual hearing, learning lip- or speech reading, and utilizing all appropriate aids seem to be the major goals (Becker 1980: 18–19).

The problems of hearing and responding are exacerbated by ordinary communication. Requests for repetitions, misinterpretations, ignoring the other person's speech, or confusing instructions and requests are frequent occurrences. This leads to irritation, frustration, or anger on the part of both persons. Gradually the hearing person begins to withdraw from all but the most essential communication with the hearing disabled and sometimes will talk to others in the presence of the hearing disabled as though they were not present.

If this pattern of communication occurs frequently, it tends to lead to embarrassment, denial, anger, anxiety, suspicion, withdrawal, isolation, and possibly to depression. Often those with hearing problems think of themselves as lesser persons and become more isolated, withdrawn, and finally depressed, at which point they give up any effort to improve the situation. If the hearing loss is coupled with other deficits, such as sight diminution, difficulties with teeth or dentures causing speech impairment, difficulty with mobility, the loss of a spouse, or the need to move from a home of many years, the effects are devastating and extremely difficult to overcome.

Successful adaptation to hearing dysfunction takes active effort by the person involved as well as by other family members. The emotions, attitudes, and actions of the family can support, aid, and encourage the one with the hearing loss; or they can ignore, thwart, hamper, disparage, or discourage attempts to communicate. These factors are amply demonstrated in the two examples that follow. They are included because they illustrate the variety and complexity of hearing dysfunction. Both were provided through records and interviews with clients of the Auditory Education Center (AEC) in June 1988.

Mr. D. was born in 1918, is married, and has two children and two brothers. He lives in a western state. He was a chemical engineer who was moving up in his company and "was slated for a top post." Activities important to him were music and singing. He used to sing solos in the church choir and often was requested as the solo singer at weddings. When his hearing problems began, his wife went back to full-time work. According to the medical records available, Mr. D.'s hearing problem began in 1934, when he began to have "dizzy periods." An aneurism was discovered in 1957 which affected the speech centers. In 1962 he had a left labyrinthectomy which helped the dizziness abate, but the surgery impaired his balance and hearing on the left side.

In 1962 Mr. D. could hear with only one ear. By 1985 he could not hear speech, and music was "horrible." His problem became much worse, and he consulted many different physicians. A hearing aid was recommended, and he attended classes at a university to adapt to it. He added that his hearing fluctuated between some understanding of speech and then none for a few months at a time. (This exacerbation and remission of hearing loss provided intermittent despair and hope, allowing him to avoid confronting the possibility of permanent hearing loss.) In 1987 he attended a speech and hearing center for five sessions which did not improve his ability. He could hardly understand people, and music was still "horrible."

Early in 1988 Mr. D.'s hearing "went out again." At that point he was admitted to the Mayo Clinic which found otosclerosis after a thorough physical examination. He was given three medications to use daily for one year and told to return for a checkup. He also was told he would never fully regain his hearing. After that Mr. D.'s brother arranged for him to come to Atlanta to attend the AEC, where this interview took place.

On the Self Evaluation Quantified Denver Scale, taken in May 1988, Mr. D.'s responses indicated confused and contradictory feelings about himself and others. (This should not be ignored in the therapeutic rehabilitative process.) He said that when he first had the aneurism, "I couldn't talk. I had to teach myself to read again, after having been a speed reader, and I had to relearn how to talk." His brother, present at the interview, added that after the aneurism there was a complete personality change. Mr. D. withdrew into his shell and only very recently began to come out of it. On the self-evaluation scale, Mr. D. said he feels very lonely due to his hearing loss, but is not negative about life in general and does not feel threatened by many communication situations. He feels he "always fits into conversations." Both the first and second time he completely lost his hearing "it hurt very very much, very badly."

Mr. D. said he expresses his frustrations and anger at his situation by taking long walks and by physically "working like crazy." Sometimes "I take it out on others, but then I get over it." When asked if he or his wife ever thought of getting psychotherapeutic help because of his problem with communication, Mr. D. said, "No. Besides I have all the help I need," indicating his brother, a psychologist. Mr. D. was asked if he considered himself a perfectionist. After thinking for a short while, he said yes, and added that he does not believe others who say his voice is alright. "I realize I will never come up to my expectations."

Mr. D. explained that his brother is helping him at home by using a bilingual dictionary through which they practice words and phrases in common usage. His sister-in-law says he seems to be both understanding and speaking better after three weeks in the AEC program, but he does not believe it. Mr. D. says there have been some changes after starting this program:

> I hear better than before and understand better. I used to vacillate before, but now I hear steadily. They [the AEC staff] fixed the hearing aid, and I've learned a new way of listening by watching face and body language. After going home I have thought of practicing and getting my wife to help me the same way my brother has.

The interview ended with my commenting that Mr. D. had been hearing, understanding, and talking with a complete stranger for a bit over an hour. We had understood and responded to one another with no problems.

Many questions come to mind from the history available and the one interview. For example, what was the marital relationship before and after the aneurism? Why did it take so many years of vacillation and problems before an accurate diagnosis was available? What is necessary to enable Mr. D. to continue his recent improvement? What would be most helpful to improve his wife's understanding and help, as well as improve their relationship. What kind of community resources should they be involved with? Are there any support groups near his home? Why don't all rehabilitative programs require participation by family members, since successful handling of this problem is also dependent on their emotions, attitudes, knowledge, and behavior?

The second person interviewed was very different as to the development of the problem and its outcome.

Mr. K. was born in 1916, has two children, and had been a fireman. After retiring from that, he worked for Eastern Airlines as a mechanic for nineteen years. He retired from that job in 1984 because of his hearing loss. "I didn't want to look like a fool asking the same questions over" while in a class to learn the use of new tools.

He had a hearing problem for about thirty years which increased very gradually. His first wife complained about it and urged a hearing test when he went for a medical exam. "The doctor said it was only a marital difference, so I tended to turn the whole thing off. About five years ago I finally decided to go to the Health Maintenance Organization, where I was referred to the ear specialist at a rehabilitation center." He was tested for a hearing aid elsewhere, and both ears were found to be marginal. At that time he was asked in which ear he heard better. Due to the cost, he was sold one hearing aid for the "worse" ear. "They were nice people; they were not trying to make a bundle of money on me."

The one hearing aid helped some but wasn't really adequate. In 1985 he heard of the Auditory Education Center and went for classes. The record indicated that initially he was found to be a poor speech reader. By the end of the course it was noted, "He follows through on suggestions, put forth effort to learn, and has a pleasant personality. He is a pleasure to work with."

Mr. K. added that a "very sharp lady" at the AEC suggested he try two hearing aids. "It was an eye opener." He also added that he was given material to read on late onset deafness. He said he was "the typical case; it described my situation perfectly. For many years I was rejecting the problem. The classes really helped. I have better insight. Also, I have to start paying attention to listening to others and stop tuning them out. Then I can hear better."

Other health problems involved removal of cataracts and glaucoma surgery with a lens implant, so he no longer needs eyeglasses. Mr. K. commented that years ago "we [hard of hearing older people] were objects of ridicule. No one would do that to blind people. Now it seems to be getting better."

During the years Mr. K. ignored and resisted his loss of hearing, which created communication problems for him. However his insight, understanding, and adaptation to and acceptance of his condition have helped considerably. After getting two hearing aids his life has improved tremendously, but some things still are annoying, such as wind noises, especially when wearing a hat. Microphones also produce extra sounds and whistling, making hearing difficult. He needs to turn his hearing aids down while speaking and listening on the telephone, because the sounds are too loud and produces whistling noises. However he has continued with most of his activities.

Mr. K's hearing loss appears to have practically no effect on his marriage, although it did during his first marriage, before the problem was recognized and handled. Mr. K. and the current Mrs. K. met at a church dance and "have been dancing ever since." The families of both accepted and were happy about the marriage.

The questions arising from Mr. K's situation relate to the history of his problem. Why was his hearing loss not discovered and treated earlier? Why are costs for hearing aids so high that even when two are needed only one is recommended, with no plans for the other? Is the response of the first physician, who termed the lack of hearing "a marital difference," a typical medical response? In both examples the attitudes of the spouses strongly affected the ways these men handled their problems.

EFFECTS ON FAMILY RELATIONSHIPS

Generalities in this area have been mentioned previously. However the actual effects of hearing disability on family life obviously differ for each family, based on the age of family members, the hearing of other members, previous family attitudes and relationships, and the health of each. A hearing spouse who has chronic pain or mobility problems may have more difficulty with the hearing disability of the other than a spouse without major health problems. Factors of control and power by the hearing spouse relate to the feeling of powerlessness and isolation in the non-hearing partner. Tensions resulting from these paradoxical feelings and from the strain of listening with eyes as well as ears and constantly needing to face the other person while talking add to fatigue and exhaustion for both (Glass 1985: 172). If these attributes are paramount in the family and not helped by aids, rehabilitative therapy, or psychosocial therapy, communication within the family becomes more constricted, leading to negative sequelae. Glass points out other factors. When talking to a lip-reader, she speaks more slowly and simply, hesitating to express complex ideas and feelings. Particularly when tired, the effort to speak clearly is more of a strain. The hearing impaired person also may be tired due to the extra effort to receive information with four senses instead of five. If a sudden change of plans is necessary, this may not be explained in advance to the hearing impaired person. This enhances the feeling of being left out by the hearing impaired person and guilt in the hearing person.

Some of the negatives mentioned seem more prevalent in Mr. D.'s situation from the one interview. When he began to have severe hearing problems, his wife went back to work full time; their children already were adults. In 1985, after getting the hearing aid, his wife did not go to the university with him to learn how to adapt to it and to the hearing loss, saying it was too far from home. Mr. D. volunteered the following: "It kinda gets to me. I have to be very careful with her. She gets angry because I don't hear or understand her. Now [after the AEC course] I feel I could help her understand my problems better." The brother added that Mr. D. gets no help at home. Mr. D. volunteered that before starting at the AEC, he did not recognize his brother's voice on the phone and this annoyed him. He also said that his wife could have divorced him because he was such a mess, but she didn't.

A very different attitude is indicated by Mr. K. and his wife. Both entered this second marriage with a chronic health problem; hers was fighting cancer for thirty years. Despite these problems, the couple had complete support and encouragement from their respective families, and both are involved in their churches and in the community. Between two pensions, "perks" as a former airline employee, Social Security, and Medicare, Mr. K. said he feels financially secure. They radiated a contentment and happiness with their lives. It is interesting to note that during the interview, Mr. K., wearing both hearing aids while facing me, also heard and responded to his wife's comments, although she was sitting to the side behind him. He seemed hardly disabled as long as he used his hearing aids.

In the literature (P. Ashley 1985: 71–75) there is a moving account by a man and his wife in separate articles of the effects of sudden hearing loss and a family's adjustment to the problems involved. Although the family is much younger than the ages considered here, some of the principles pointed out by the wife in dealing with the

problem can be applied to older people, and therefore are para-
phrased here:

1. There is strain on every family member, no matter what
   the age, when the deafness first occurs. Children and
   grandchildren also are affected.

2. There needs to be easy communication within the family.
   It is important for the deaf person to remain closely involved in all aspects of family life, aware of the trivial as
   well as the important events.

3. Lip or speech reading is the main form of communication
   with the rest of the world.

4. With words that are difficult to lip-read, write them out or
   spell them quickly to keep the momentum of conversation
   going.

5. Fatigue of the deaf person influences conversation. It is
   more difficult to speech read when tired.

6. When minor emergencies occur, try to explain to the deaf
   one as soon as possible.

7. Any leisure activity that involves physical exertion is a very
   positive way of maintaining social contacts as well as healthy
   bodily functioning. Visual entertainment instead of verbal
   drama or music is something the deaf person can share fully
   with family and others.

8. Deafness alters the domestic role of hearing members also,
   especially when the deaf family member requires the presence of the hearing ones.

9. Sometimes people avoid talking directly to the deaf one and
   instead talk to the hearing companion. The hearing companion often can offset this by keeping the eyes focused on
   the face of the deaf one, or suggesting that it is easier for
   the deaf one to understand if you look directly at him or
   her.

10. Any assistance should be done with consideration and tact.

11. The self-confidence of the deaf person is an important fac-
    tor in its management. Is the lack of hearing a problem to

be handled as easily as possible or a handicap that prevents full functioning?

A most sensitive account of the feelings of a hearing person in the family of a deaf husband and sons is "And Sarah Laughed" (Greenberg 1982: 158–175). In this short story Sarah expresses her isolation because of her inability to communicate hopes, fears, plans, and joys with her family. It describes how the family eventually was able to overcome communication problems.

In both Ashley's account of a real family and the short story the strong point is made that the hearing members need to adapt to the non-hearing one(s), just as the non-hearing person needs to adapt to the problem. One hopes rehabilitation specialists are aware of this and include family members and/or care givers in the rehabilitation process. The short story addresses the feelings of control that the hearing one may have. What does this do to the person who may have had more control before the loss of hearing? Is there a need for both parties to provide input in family affairs, both trivial and important? Is there a need for education and counseling of both partners to understand each other's needs so their life together can be as rich as possible? It seems that both partners might need help in learning how to help others—family, friends, and incidental persons—communicate. Can family support groups, Family Life Education sessions, or family therapy with audiologists and social workers as coleaders be helpful in this area?

EFFECTS ON PEER RELATIONSHIPS

Obviously substantial diminution of hearing affects relationships among friends, because communication is a mutual process. In the book *What Do I Do Now? Problems and Adaptations of the Deafened Adult,* the authors speak directly to the affected person:

> It is possible that some of your friends may be unable to understand the intensity of your experience. . . . They will tend to . . . tell you to cheer up because things cannot be that bad, or avoid you altogether. . . . Sometimes, family or friends are guilty of denying the deafened person's hearing loss. In this case, denial reflects *their* inability to deal with the facts of deafness . . .

they impede their own acceptance as well as that of the deafened person. (Louey & Per-Lee 1983: 6, 11)

Most of the authors discuss a falling away of some friends and a tendency among the newly deafened to retreat rather than striving to remain connected to the hearing world. Kaplan (1985: 86) points out that

Motivation is related to lifestyles. The person who is active physically, mentally, and emotionally and participates in community affairs, and who perhaps retains some employment, needs to communicate and will have a strong desire to adjust to amplification. The withdrawn person who spends most of his time alone usually will not—unless he depends on the telephone and television.

Another author, focusing on prelingually deaf people, states, "My major thesis is that . . . an individual learns to cope early in life with a marginal social status." He discusses the deaf clubs that sometimes function as closed societies. If they meet in the evening, this effectively prevents older people, many of whom don't like to go out after dark, from attending. Members often are impatient with those who can't communicate by signing, which effectively prevents the newly deaf from participating (Becker 1980: 6, 70).

Among those who lose hearing postlingually, the age at onset, the severity and rapidity of loss, and the residual hearing all make for a variety of subgroups (Meadow-Orlans 1985: 36).

There seems to be a resistance among older people who lose hearing to identify with other deaf people. They have been part of the hearing world for many years and don't want to separate from it. The stigma, for them and their cohorts who grew up in a world where disabilities made one "inferior," is still too strong.

Most of the authors researched did not mention or question the quantity and quality of peer relationships the newly hard of hearing had before the problem arose. Any comparison of friendships and peer relationships must relate to the before and after in that person's life and life-style to provide any degree of accuracy.

An astute comment about the relationship with one's colleagues and peers is provided by another author:

There was an interesting difference in the attitude of Members of Parliament compared with that of constituents. The MPs on all sides were friendly enough, yet there was an obvious wariness about some of them. Some were willing to cooperate, but unwilling to initiate. If I approached them they would always respond, but that would be the end of the matter. I was perceiving for the first time the polite, but restrained reactions of colleagues who had no wish to wound, but no wish to help. (J. Ashley 1985: 64)

Is it possible that older people with hearing problems sense this kind of courteous but distant approach by colleagues and friends? Is it possible that the reluctance of so many to adapt to their deafness is related to such awareness?

In recent years there has been much more openness, public awareness, and discussion of hearing loss than previously. Is it possible that public awareness and increased knowledge, achievements of public figures known to be deaf, the Theatre of the Deaf, and the public image of Gallaudet College are gradually changing people's thinking about those with limited or no hearing? Is it possible that as more and more people publicly use hearing aids this aid may become as "acceptable" as eyeglasses?

In attempting to separate effects of this disability on friends and peers from its effects on activities of social functioning there is bound to be a good deal of overlap. The social life of adults frequently is integrated into their communal activities.

Let's look again at Mr. D., this time in connection with his friends. He responded on the Quantified Denver Scale that he mildly disagreed with the following statement: "People sometimes avoid me due to hearing disability." He did agree that he is no longer comfortable in new social settings. However, during the interview he stated that he is not threatened by many communication situations and always fits into conversations. He still has trouble going outside and talking to people, although he now can handle shopping. His brother said he withdrew into his shell and only recently began to come out of it. His professional colleagues and friends in the church choir fell away. Mr. D. mentioned only one friend who continued contact.

Mr. K., on the other hand, had a gradual onset of his hearing problem, which he denied for a number of years with the "help" of his physician. He resigned from his last job because he did not want to make a fool of himself before his colleagues and the instructor when he had to request many repetitions. He told them why he was retiring at that time. One hearing aid was helpful to Mr. K., and the second almost wiped out his problem. Even when using only one Mr. K. was drawn into social life with his second wife's family.

Mr. K. said the hearing problem affected his social life. He no longer attends Knights of Columbus meetings because the acoustics are so bad, and he still cannot hear the sermons in church. An additional note is that Mr. K. tried to help his neighbor by suggesting that he should have his hearing tested, and used himself as an example. The neighbor insisted he needed no help and hears only what he wants to hear. Mr. K. said this was foolish.

Mr. K. made new acquaintances and friends through his community activities, to be discussed later, and through membership in new groups, including an alumni club of former airline employees which has periodic group trips at minimal cost. Mr. K. also enjoys working in his garden and fixing up his house.

ACTIVITIES OF SOCIAL FUNCTIONING

Much has been written of the importance of social networks for older people, but without reference to late onset deafness. An important exception is a two-part national study on programs and services for the hearing impaired elderly in the United States. A survey of 13,932 senior centers, clubs, and programs was conducted to identify those serving the hearing impaired elderly. Almost 7,000 responded, and 344 indicated that they had programs, activities, and services especially designed for the hard-of-hearing elderly. The community centers were further divided into those where the hearing impaired were mainstreamed and those for the hearing impaired only, with significant differences found between them in all areas except supplying information (Sela 1986: Abstract III). This is the first study on a national basis of participation by the hard-of-hearing elderly in senior centers, clubs, and programs. As such it provides an impetus for further exploration and research.

Aside from the writing by both Ashleys (1985), the literature reviewed did not seem to indicate individuals dealing with this area.

The examples used here indicate how different the social life-style of the hard-of-hearing elderly can be.

Mr. D.'s social life was deeply affected by his problem. He no longer goes to church because he cannot hear the sermon and the music is so "horrible." He can no longer sing at weddings. His employment was cut short. He no longer attends professional meetings and conferences. His use of the telephone is curtailed. He did not recognize his brother's voice on the phone. He does not understand closed captioning and therefore has much difficulty watching TV.

However Mr. D. does function in other areas. He does the shopping and now reads some professional journals and the papers. He is kept "pretty busy taking care of my place and the rentals we have." He loves to drive and take long automobile trips. He votes. He did not mention the loss of friends but, from his brother, very few are still involved with him. Mr. D.'s experience of searching out physicians and audiologic specialists to find a solution to his problem indicates the need for consideration by specialists of the total person. Those he consulted seemed to have handled only the immediate problem. Did that occur because they responded only to the expressed needs, or because they saw only the expressed need as their concern? As with any disability, the expressed need often is all the individual can grasp, but the disability is only one part of the total person who needs help.

On the other hand, Mr. K. is very active in the community despite his hearing loss. The only thing he no longer does is attend Knights of Columbus meetings. He and his wife go dancing, although not as often as before their marriage. They both participate as drivers in a meals-on-wheels program for shut-in people. If the home they deliver to needs some small repairs, they come back at another time to tend to it. Their traveling opportunities come through the alumni club of former airline employees. Mr. K. still goes to union meetings, where he sits up front in order to hear adequately, and still goes to church, although he does not hear the sermons. He was asked to attend one hard-of-hearing group as "a shining example." He said only some of the people there could lip-read. The K.'s live in a small suburban community and said there are no support groups for the hard of hearing there. He checks out the local newspaper for announcements of group meetings like Alcoholics Anonymous, but has not found any for the hearing impaired.

The Auditory Education Center, still developing its programs, is planning to initiate a social group for mid-life adults with hearing loss because the director feels that services for this age range are lacking.

PROFESSIONAL FUNCTIONS OUTSIDE JOB LIMITS

Self-help groups have grown tremendously since the 1970s. Some of the reasons for this are indicated by Warner (1987: 237–238) in his summary of Deaf Services Centers in Region IV of the U.S. Department of Education. Naisbitt (1982: 150) explains it differently as one of the megatrends. He equates medical self-help groups as part of the thrust away from the medical establishment. He points out that "self-help groups bring peers together for mutual assistance in satisfying a common need . . . when the self-help model is adapted in neighborhoods or communities, however, personal self-help becomes social activism. And socially oriented self-help groups are active all across the country." This concept spread also to people with disabilities: The Disabled Veterans of America, the Alzheimer's Disease and Related Disorders Association (ADRDA), and Self-Help for the Hard of Hearing (SHHH; the example used for organization involvement below).

It is encouraging to note that a 1987 textbook for audiologists not only lists ancillary personnel but includes a chapter on their functions. It also suggests ways audiologists might work with them in the rehabilitation of elderly hard of hearing (Garstecki: 429–458).

The ancillary personnel suggested include the family physician, the otologist, the dispenser of hearing aids and other devices, the psychologist, the social worker, the registered nurse, activity and retirement community center staff, the vocational counselor, and the other family members. Consumer groups and government special service programs also are included. The importance of good eyesight and visual acuity in the auditory rehabilitation process is the first factor discussed (after the auditory factors). In view of this, it is interesting to note that neither ophthalmologists nor optometrists are included among the ancillary personnel. The chapter on the hearing impaired geriatric client makes the point that visual messages relate clues that are very helpful. This leads to the conclusion that "therapy undertaken with older hearing impaired individuals should be done with a bisensory approach" (McCarthy 1987: 399).

The example in this section is a state self-help group which came together for networking and advocacy for themselves and others, provided in an interview with the key social worker.

A professional social worker at the area school for deaf and hearing impaired children—hearing impaired herself—began to stimulate other professionals at the same school to organize the Georgia Council for the Hearing Impaired, composed of both professionals and hearing impaired lay people throughout the state. The purpose was to secure needed services for the whole hearing impaired community. This group needed to educate and secure the cooperation of legislators and other appropriate heads of human service agencies both public and private in order to proceed. The Deaf Services Center they hope to see established may seem to be exclusionary, but it will be instrumental locally in the fuller integration of hearing impaired into the hearing community.

There has been a Governor's Council for Developmental Disabilities for people up to the age of twenty-two only. The social worker learned from colleagues that they had tried previously, with the hearing population, to initiate a self-help advocacy group for deaf and hard-of-hearing adults on a statewide basis. It had not worked because, it appeared, those contacted were not ready to network. Three colleagues also felt the need for an advocacy network and were willing to continue to develop this idea. Feedback was received from the deaf staff at the school, who voted unanimously to develop a statewide advocacy effort. The superintendent of the school, sensitive to the need for community services by staff, allowed some time for this. The staff started to network by involving people in their own communities first. They then contacted other appropriate professionals throughout the state to work toward a legislative breakfast in January 1987. The purpose was to acquaint legislators and state officials with the needs of the deaf and hearing impaired, who carry this problem into adulthood. Three hundred hearing impaired people from around the state and thirty legislators attended this first communal activity. This was the first time there had been such cooperation among this group for a communal project.

One result of this experience was the support of the Commissioner of Human Resources and the Director of the Department of Rehabilitation Services. In addition, two legislators indicated their support and sponsorship of the proposal for a community services center for the hearing impaired, commonly known as a deaf service center.

Members of the deaf community at the first legislative breakfast formed themselves into the Georgia Council for the Hearing Impaired, elected officers, and began to meet monthly. They get out a newsletter and refined their proposal (which was submitted too late to be considered in that legislative session). They also are applying for federal block grant money to help start up the deaf service center. There is no paid staff, and volunteers are scattered throughout the state.

The second draft of the proposal (1988), shared here by the Georgia Council for the Hearing Impaired with written permission, indicated there were approximately 395,000 hearing impaired individuals of all ages in Georgia, and this was the only southeastern state without a deaf service center. It further pointed out that "the State of Georgia is currently unable to meet the needs of the deaf community" and other community services throughout the state cannot "provide services appropriately and effectively."

The objectives of the center were listed as an education and consultation resource; development of statewide community involvement; provide outreach, counseling, and support services; and coordination and networking/linkage services. The eight goals of the service center were very varied:

1. Advocate for the development of a TDD/TTY telephone relay service so the deaf and hard of hearing can communicate with each other and with the hearing community, thereby having equal access to services available to all. This tends to enhance independence and privacy for those using this communication device.

2. Attempt to influence the development of more and better opportunities for community programs and specialized services. It also will use counseling, crisis intervention, and assessment as needed, and determine if referral to another facility is needed.

3. Serve as a statewide clearinghouse for information on deafness and for programs and services for the deaf community.

4. Promote public awareness of deafness and the special needs of the deaf and hearing impaired.

5. Establish a framework for consultation and cooperation with community agencies and organizations dealing with the hearing impaired population and their significant others.

6. Work in cooperation with the Georgia Association of the Deaf and the Georgia Registry for Interpreters of the Deaf.

7. Serve as a liaison with state agencies to facilitate mutual interaction, coordination, and integration of programs and services.

8. Facilitate a program of classes, workshops, and other activities for the welfare of citizens concerned with deafness.

In a follow-up contact with the president of the Council for the Hearing Impaired, it was learned that a center is planned for the state. In the future it hopes to establish centers in several cities. They will attempt to identify and accommodate all hearing impaired, including the elderly, through public relations and outreach to schools, family and service agencies, nursing homes, and hearing aid dealers. The council also is planning to provide education to those same groups to try to overcome the resistance of older people with hearing problems to secure appropriate help.

This self-help group started with a statewide advocacy and education focus. The service center, which is to provide consultation to other organizations, advocacy, education, and some services to the hearing impaired, is the first project. This is, perhaps, a more complex and sophisticated approach than self-help and support groups that start with support and direct services only to affected families and individuals.

A Regional Representative for the U.S. Department of Education, Region IV, before his retirement, was involved in a survey of community services centers for deaf people, which found continuing interest in how and where such centers can be established with the greatest potential of helping the deaf and hard of hearing. He felt a strong interest may be present because of five basic changes occurring nationwide:

1. Recognition of the right of access to public services for the deaf and hearing impaired
2. Advances in the transmission of electronic messages
3. Philosophical changes in education; that is, the movement to mainstream deaf children
4. An increase in the number of trained interpreters
5. The aging of the United States population, leading to a greater proportion of hearing impaired individuals (Warner 1987: 237–238).

ORGANIZATION OR INSTITUTION INVOLVEMENT

The development, goals, characteristics, and major functions of organizations are outlined in the previous chapter.

When any one organization attempts to cover all aspects of a particular disease, new organizations may be created to focus on more limited aspects which the organizers feel are not being adequately addressed. This also operates in the reverse. When it is felt that national organizations have too limited a scope and do not address other important aspects, another organization is created to address those needs. Such was the situation with Self-Help for the Hard of Hearing (SHHH), founded by Howard E. Stone. (All material on the development of SHHH comes from his 1985 article and a telephone conference in 1988.)

Stone describes his own hearing impairment during his adult life and his frustration with finding (after his retirement) any organization to help him. He felt the purposes of the Consumers Organization for the Hearing Impaired, founded in 1977, were too technical and that it was too limited to involve its hard-of-hearing members. John Gardner of Common Cause advised Stone "to establish an independent organization devoted to self-help." He started with a small group of hearing impaired people, using an audio loop. In 1979 an article about Stone's career with the CIA briefly mentioned the formation of SHHH. This generated many letters of inquiry which encouraged him to continue.

The original concept was for SHHH to be an organization with very low dues, including the widest possible membership of older people living on fixed incomes, whose local chapters would have great autonomy. Enhancing the human spirit was the initial focus; hearing impairment would be treated as only one of life's crises. The national office was to disseminate information to local chapters about methods and tools of communication. The preamble to the SHHH constitution establishes that impaired hearing often leads to loneliness and that patterns of community life basically ignore this problem. It then states: "Our primary purpose, then, is to educate ourselves, our relatives and our friends about the cause, nature, complications and possible remedies of hearing loss."

Stone used every opportunity open to him to expand the audience for his message—working full time, getting articles published in a variety of media, speaking wherever requested and insisting on local media coverage for each speech, and speaking at hearings of national legislative committees. Over a three-year period he spoke in twenty-four states, Canada, and Australia, which resulted in twenty-one SHHH chapters. Meanwhile, his articles in *Modern Maturity* (the AARP magazine) resulted in thousands of inquiries. He also began the *SHHH Journal* which was sent to all who inquired. Further publicity resulted in three one-hour TV programs on hearing loss for Public Broadcasting.

Stone learned that the 1981 White House Conference on Aging was being planned without any references to either the deaf or the hard of hearing. Arthur Fleming (former Secretary of the Department of Health, Education and Welfare) was instrumental in arranging a meeting between Stone and the conference staff in October 1980, which resulted in Stone's being asked to organize a miniconference on elderly hearing impaired people and produce a report by February 1981. Although eight organizations agreed to sponsor this conference, three that contributed more than just their name were the American Speech-Language-Hearing Association, the National Association of the Deaf, and the Alexander Graham Bell Association for the Deaf. Professionals around the country were contacted, and all agreed to participate. SHHH offered to pay the expenses of consumers invited to attend. The manufacturers of four major sound systems provided free equipment. The National Institute on Aging provided a five-thousand-dollar research grant, but SHHH was deeply in debt until the Administration on Aging provided additional funds. The mini-conference produced a report, published by the Government Printing Office. It stated that hard-of-hearing people were much less informed than the deaf on subjects of vital importance to them. Four recommendations resulted from the conference:

1. Publish a consumer's guide to alternative hearing devices listing what is available, where to find it, what it costs, and how it is used.

2. Develop and conduct programs for service providers and consumers on hearing devices, alternative communication methods, and related information.

3. Assist local and state organizations (such as AAAs, service clubs, and libraries) to provide audiovisual information and demonstration centers for the hearing impaired.

4. Encourage captioned public television programs. Over the years SHHH began to try to implement the recommendations, particularly numbers 1 and 3.

As SHHH grew in membership, local chapters were encouraged to develop. The chapters and *SHHH News*, the newsletter, link members to the national office and help to implement programs in the local communities.

Open chapter meetings and an atmosphere of welcoming all is encouraged. However, this can create difficulties because chapters can have a mix of prelingually deaf, hard-of-hearing, deafened, and hearing members. Those deaf from childhood may have speech difficulties which are difficult for lip-readers to understand. Some sign while they talk, which often is distracting to lip-readers. All people, including the prelingually deaf, are welcome as long as they accept SHHH's purpose and philosophy, remembering it was formed for and seeks primarily to serve hard-of-hearing people.

In the 10 years of its existence (in 1985), SHHH had grown tremendously. What are some of the factors influencing this growth? Was it an idea whose time had come? Was it the growth in the number of older people with hearing problems? Was it the initial encouragement of people on the national scene who helped open doors for Stone's idea? Was it the devotion and steadiness of volunteers who worked for years without pay to help move the organization forward? Was it the personality and drive of Howard Stone? Stone has seen burgeoning interest in hard-of-hearing adults by Gallaudet University and the National Association of the Deaf. Some congressmen are showing awareness, and new groups are forming for adults with hearing problems.

Stone's goals for SHHH are all-encompassing. He feels that in the future (after 1985) SHHH needs to continue to grow in numbers, importance, and influence, but individuals must remain the first priority. SHHH should advocate for the deaf as well as the hard of hearing because legislation that helps one group also can help the other. SHHH also should work closely with industry to improve the quality and lower the cost of remedial aids. It should press for more research on the prevention and treatment of hearing loss; sponsor forums and provide information on hearing health; endorse and help to implement policies to integrate hard-of-hearing persons better into our society and work force; stimulate research in neglected areas; provide materials and services to help hard-of-hearing persons their families and friends better relate to each other; and strive to enrich the lives of hard-of-hearing people with varied activities suited to their condition and preferences.

Some of the Stone's future goals for SHHH are very broad, such as helping hard-of-hearing people who are abused, victimized, or defrauded and raising funds for research. Will the diffusion of goals dilute the effectiveness of the organization in its primary focus of service and programs for individuals? Has the already broadening focus opened a gap between local chapters and the national organization? At what point does the size of an organization result in a changed focus? When this happens, is there a qualitative change in the organization, and is there a time and function lag between the original purpose and the new ones? Can an organization with broad national objectives also maintain its direct services and warm support for individuals?

An interesting and useful form of organizational involvement with hearing impairment is a series of pamphlets, written by experts in their own fields, sponsored by the American Speech-Language-Hearing Association and the National Information Center on Deafness of Gallaudet University (Williams 1987: 1–3; Wax & DiPietro 1987: 1–5). The pamphlets focus on understanding the realities of hearing loss in adulthood and suggest practical adjustments to that loss for hearing impaired persons, their families, friends, and the professionals who serve them. They might be used by other organizations for public education, thus avoiding duplication of effort and financial resources.

GOVERNMENT INVOLVEMENT

In 1991 loss of hearing among older people was, among men, second only to arthritis in prevalence; and among women it was third in prevalence after arthritis and heart disease (Adams & Benson 1992: Table 63, 96–97). Yet despite this prevalence, there appears to be little recognition of it by federal governmental bodies interested in the social welfare of the elderly. Among the most obvious reasons are the following:

1. Hearing disability is not "dramatic" and usually does not result in death, as do Alzheimer's disease and AIDS.

2. For many years there has been a social stigma attached to deafness, which many older people have self-incorporated and, therefore, are reluctant to admit having this problem.

3. Lack of hearing is not immediately obvious to the casual observer, as is the lack of mobility. Many consider it an "invisible" problem.

4. There are numerous national organizations involved in one or more aspects of hearing deficits: the American Speech-Language-Hearing Association, American Tinnitus Association, National Information Center on Deafness, Gallaudet University, National Association of the Deaf, Alexander Graham Bell Association for the Deaf, Oral Deaf Adult Section, Self-Help for the Hard of Hearing (SHHH), to name a few. Only SHHH has established a nationwide organization that strongly advocates and pressures for education about older people with hearing loss from both the public and private sectors.

5. Much more has been done publicly over the years to help those with prelingual or childhood deafness.

6. It is only recently that the aging network at the federal and

state levels has become involved in chronic disabilities such as Alzheimer's, mental retardation, and blindness. Usually education and collaboration has come about through the efforts of the national organizations for the specific disability or their local affiliates.

For these reasons it has been difficult to find an appropriate example of federal involvement with late onset hearing disability. Therefore, this section looks at guidelines for disbursement of selected federal discretionary funds under the Department of Health and Human Services (DHH) Administration on Aging (AoA) in fiscal year 1988.

A history of the Older Americans Act (OAA), the Administration of Aging, and the aging network by Rich and Baum (1984) summarizes its goals and functioning since its inception, very abbreviated here:

The goal of establishing a central agency at the federal level that would be responsible for all programs affecting the elderly has proved impossible to realize. There are simply too many congressional committees and government departments controlling relevant areas of activity to permit this coordination. The AoA has to manage . . . by making special agreements with other bureaus that control programs for the aging outside its jurisdiction. . . . The status of programs for the aging has been subject to a number of forces working against their coordination. (48–49)

It was only in 1988, in Georgia, that two bills were passed relating to hard-of-hearing adults. One permitted speech-language pathologists and audiologists to perform hearing tests as part of the workplace hearing conservation program, and the other authorized the Department of Human Resources to establish the Service Center for Hearing Impaired Persons.

The Federal Register (December 30, 1987: 49253) provided goals and objectives of the AoA and guidelines for grant requests in fiscal year 1988. The DHH encompasses the AoA; Administration for Children, Youth and Families; Administration on Developmental Disabilities; Administration for Native Americans; and the Office of Human Developmental Services (HDS).

The Office of HDS enumerated goals shared by the four program administrations. They "share a common mission: to reduce dependency and increase self-sufficiency among our most vulnerable citizens . . . progress toward it will help more Americans live independent lives, and in the end it will reduce demand for services." It also states that public policy now articulates that "decisions are best made at the level of government closest to the target population served" (Federal Register, December 30, 1987: 49252–49253). It is possible, then, that this may result in fifty different decisions about policies and programs which address the same need.

The Administration on Aging is mandated to be the focal point and advocate for the elderly within the Department of Health and Human Services and with other federal departments and agencies. It also provides guidance and assistance to the states and communities in the development and implementation of comprehensive and coordinated service systems for older persons. The AoA's long-range objectives stated in this announcement were to stimulate systems changes to enhance family- and community-based care; promote the adoption of healthy life-styles among the elderly; provide services to the elderly in greatest need; promote preparation for an aging society; and assist state and Area Agencies on Aging and tribal organizations in carrying out their leadership roles in planning, coordinating, and assuring the availability of services for the elderly.

The major research, demonstration, development, and training efforts of the AoA are carried out through Title IV, which authorizes a program of discretionary grants and contracts to support these efforts. The AoA accomplishes its goals and objectives by working with

> state and Area Agencies on Aging, nonprofit, voluntary and philanthropic organizations and local communities, through analyzing trends and anticipating social issues that will become paramount in the future; improving the effectiveness and efficiency of services to the elderly by developing new techniques and approaches to deal with social issues; and by developing alternatives to traditional social service approaches.

It is expected that the state and Area Agencies on Aging will play critical leadership roles as catalysts, brokers, and coordinators in developing family- and community-based care for older persons. The AoA encourages applicants to include special needs of minority elders and to involve "a high degree of collaboration among state, area and local agencies as appropriate, and agencies representing minority concerns" (Federal Register, December 30, 1987: 49253).

It is helpful to analyze the goals and methods for their internal consistency and whether or not the goals can be carried out using the focus in the Federal Register. The AoA is responsible to the director of the Office of Human Services Development, not to the secretary of Health and Human Services. The Office of Human Services Development has adopted the criteria on family policy set forth by President Reagan, which is in direct conflict with some of the goals of the Older American Act (see the Federal Register, December 30, 1987: 49252–49253). Additionally, goals of the Office of Human Services Development include the statement, "will help more Americans live independent lives, and *in the end it will reduce demand for services*" (emphasis added). This appears to discount all the demographic and statistical facts of the past and projected future numbers of very old and frail elderly with chronic problems.

One further concern needs to be mentioned. The Older Americans Act and the AoA were set up to address the social concerns of the older population, such as housing, income, and employment opportunities, "the best possible physical and mental health which science can make available without regard to economic status, full restorative services, efficient community services which provide social assistance, retirement in health, dignity and honor, freedom, independence and the free exercise of individual initiative" (Rich & Baum 1984: 48–49). These were the original ideals, most of which have not yet and may never be fully realized. It is interesting to note that the guidelines and goals enumerated in the Federal Register for FY 1988 make no mention of physical and/or mental health, yet most social service and health care workers and educators in gerontology and geriatrics are aware of the interdependence of social and health factors in the well-being of the elderly. Support and rectification of problems in either area results in some relief in the other. The only mention of health factors in the AoA objectives enumerated in the Federal Register is the presidential guideline encouraging and promoting healthy lifestyles among the elderly.

Three methods the federal government and its agencies have to effect systems changes vis-à-vis the lives of the elderly are legislation, funding (Social Security and Medicare), and the disbursement of discretionary grants that promulgate standards to which the grantees must adhere. When the president and the Office of Human Services Development abdicate their responsibility to set standards and policies by saying "decisions are best made at the level of government closest to the target population served," this does not necessarily effect change.

Despite the drawbacks noted, the AoA, over the years of its existence, has encouraged and introduced incremental changes which have been very helpful to older people. One example has been the Medicaid waivers enabling states to implement in-home services for the poor elderly who otherwise are at risk of nursing home institutionalization at Medicaid expense. Another positive thrust are the senior centers and nutrition sites established under Title III, the community services part of the act, which reach many healthy older people. Home-delivered meals to the homebound elderly lag far behind the congregate meal sites, Yet isn't proper nutrition also important for health?

The federal body that was set up in 1973 to evaluate policies relating to the elderly was the Federal Council on the Aging. Its place in the hierarchy of agencies was tenuous until the 1978 amendments to the OAA, which provided for the council to have its own staff to carry out its functions. Then it concentrated mainly on the status of the frail and rural elderly and on evaluating the programs conducted under the OAA. In 1981 its funds were cut by more than half, and there was a substantial reduction in staff (Rich & Baum 1984: 51).

In our country it appears that federal and state policies and programs for the elderly exist and function based on many factors, including the ideologies of the politicians in office.

HEALTH INSURANCE: PUBLIC

Late onset hearing disability has received comparatively little attention from health insurance, both public and private. This may be due in part to the lack of a strong national organization (similar to the American Foundation for the Blind, the Arthritis Foundation, or the Alzheimer's Association) to educate and advocate publicly and widely. The lack of interest also may be due in part to the reluctance of those with late onset hearing disability to accept this as a problem that can be ameliorated. It is hoped that Self-Help for the Hard of Hearing (SHHH) will fill this gap.

Medicare does not reimburse for hearing aids or for examinations related to prescribing, fitting, or changing them (*The Medicare Handbook* 1990: 12). The *Medicaid Guide* mentions help for hearing problems in persons over age twenty-one only through the provision of hearing aids to assist or replace bodily functions (p. 8). This author was assured by the office of the state insurance commissioner (during an interview in June 1989) that health maintenance organizations will evaluate a patient's hearing on request and *may* reimburse for treatment to cure, but not for enhancement and personal adjustment. Is it possible that hearing loss can be rectified without personal adjustment and enhancement? The same resource also indicated that private insurers will provide reimbursement following ear surgery, and that health maintenance organizations also may provide more service for this disability.

Because of the lack of insurance specifically related to late onset hearing loss, this section will focus on the two main public health insurances, Medicare and Medicaid.

For many years before 1965 there had been discussion and dissention about some form of government-sponsored health protection for all persons. When it was clear that Congress would not approve a comprehensive plan to cover all citizens, an incremental approach was proposed to start with coverage for older people through Medicare. Medicare was intended to provide universal health benefits for the elderly (Rich & Baum 1984: 132).

There was powerful opposition from the American Medical Association in the 1960s, even to this incremental governmental involvement in health care. In order to reduce this important opposition, "there was to be no interference with the normal means of payment for the services of physicians" (Rich & Baum 1984: 133).

Federal involvement in health care after 1965 consisted of four parts:

1. The Hill-Burton Hospital Survey and Construction Act of 1946 provided for upgrading and construction of new hos-

pitals in states that agreed to the guidelines. After 1954 this was extended to nursing homes that could be linked to hospitals.

2. Medicare, Part A, is a compulsory hospital insurance program linked directly to Social Security and financed through a payroll tax. It covers many expenses while a person is hospitalized.

3. Medicare, Part B, is voluntary insurance available to those who have Part A. Part B is financed in part by the federal government and in part by monthly premiums paid by those who receive Social Security. It covers a limited number of health care costs including outpatient physician fees and some other outpatient costs.

4. Medicaid is a joint federal-state assistance program aimed at providing for the medical needs of the financially eligible aged and others. It includes long-term nursing home costs for the needy.

The federal government pays intermediaries such as Blue Cross and commercial insurance companies to administer Medicare and to contract with service providers. By 1980 there were seventy-five intermediaries throughout the country for Part A of Medicare.

Almost as soon as the federal involvement began, health care and hospital costs started to rise, often faster than inflation rates. "The initial assumption that the fiscal intermediaries would exercise extensive cost controls proved to be in error. As a consequence, abuses were frequent" (Rich & Baum 1984: 155).

Over the decades there have been numerous changes and amendments to Medicare, most of which has resulted in ever-increasing premiums for Part B and larger proportions of coinsurance, payable by the patient for Part A. These changes were designed to lower Medicare costs as the consumer paid more. Other measures sequentially instituted to lower Medicare costs included the Professional Standards Review Organization (PSRO) in 1972, which had officials of hospitals reviewing their own hospitals. This was not very effective in reducing costs. Dissatisfaction with this plan led, in 1982, to the establishment of the non–hospital based Peer Review Organization (PRO), which was similar to its predecessor. However, changes in the Social Security Act in 1983 required hospitals "to contract with the PROs for review of admissions, quality of care and other matters" (Rich & Baum 1984: 140). Diagnostic related groups (DRG) introduced in 1983 set limits to the length of stay in hospitals for 470 categories of ill health (Health Care Financing Administration, 1987 pamphlet, 1–5). Under this plan hospitals would not be reimbursed by Medicare for inpatient stays longer than those stipulated, except in extraordinary situations. Physicians who "do not comply may be terminated" (Leyerle 1984: 103–104). This led to concern among many that patients would be discharged before recovery was adequate. This criticism was so strong that the Health Care Financing Administration (HCFA) published and sent to all Medicare beneficiaries the pamphlet "Your Hospital Stay under Medicare's Prospective Payment System," to reassure potential patients. All these changes have resulted in higher copayments by and more limited services to Medicare beneficiaries. In addition the encroaching privatization of the health care industry led to cost consciousness and restructuring pressures to keep profits at high levels (Ginzberg 1985: 191–192; Leyerle 1984: 166).

The most recent attempt to change Medicare was the Catastrophic Care Coverage Act, signed into law in June 1988 but rescinded in the fall of 1989. The American Association of Retired Persons (AARP), although not advocating a national health care act, was urging broader Medicare coverage for older people with catastrophic health care costs.

Without going into specifics about who and what this act covered and how it would have been financed (primarily by the age group it purported to help), suffice it to say that it represented an important change in the Medicare insurance system, with repercussions for private health insurance. It is important to note the lack of Medicare coverage both before and after the catastrophic provisions for comparatively inexpensive health aids such as eyeglasses, dental care and dentures, and hearing aids, which alleviate but do not cure health problems. Medicare does help pay for expensive internal organ transplants and durable medical equipment such as leg braces. However, sight, dental care, and hearing also are essential to the functioning of older people and can help to prevent more costly health problems.

Whatever form changes in public payment for health care take, whether as changes in Medicare and Medicaid or as a national health care plan, questions ought to be raised about all new costs and coverages as part of an evaluation of all proposed legislation:

1. What proportion of older people are expected to be helped by this bill?

2. What proportion of older people are expected to be hurt financially by this bill?

3. Which groups in the health care industry profit by the various provisions?

4. Have its provisions fostered consolidation of aspects of the health care industry into even larger corporate bodies?

5. Are there any provisions for capping profits or profit rates of private suppliers and providers of health care? If not, why not?

6. Have its provisions fostered new providers of health care or maintained independent groups?

7. Can the ever-increasing costs to both the government and Medicare beneficiaries be borne only by both groups, especially as the number and proportion of older people continue to increase?

8. What new resources, techniques, and methods of financing and administering health care does this plan consider?

9. Can the philosophical basis and cost of Medicare be compared with similar factors in the health care of older people in countries such as Canada, Great Britain, Denmark, Germany, or Sweden?

These kinds of questions need to be resolved whether or not a national health care plan for the United States, covering all citizens, is proposed.

Medicaid for financially needy persons was enacted in the same year as Medicare, to replace the categories of aid to the disabled, aged, and blind. Medicaid is more variable than Medicare because it is financed jointly by federal and state monies with state variations of eligibility requirements and health problems covered. Traditionally it has covered more health care needs than Medicare. Some states may include services other states and the federal government exclude if the person qualifies under a means test. The family is permitted to keep its home and a very limited amount of income with which to function. Medicaid also covers those who require medical assistance only (MAO), the medically needy, and those already receiving Supplemental Security Income (SSI) and Aid to Families with Dependent Children (AFDC) (Rich & Baum, 1984: 141–143).

Like Medicare, Medicaid has undergone many incremental changes, particularly new constraints, since its inception. The federal involvement includes certain mandatory services and categories of people to receive them, while providing the states with options for additional services and other categories of people, including those who can "spend down" for Medicaid eligibility. Thus, Medicaid coverage and services will differ from state to state (Newcomer, Benjamin, & Sattler 1985: 69).

It appears that most states maintained or expanded benefit packages between the mid-1970s and 1982. After the Office of Budget Reconciliation Act of 1981 (OBRA) many states experienced budget deficits and made major reductions in Medicaid benefits, restricting a number of optional benefits including dentures for adults, hearing aids and batteries, and eyeglass replacements. A few states also eliminated the nonemergency transportation option which had been available for medical and rehabilitation treatment appointments (Harrington et al. 1985: 85–86).

By 1982 public expenditures by both Medicare and Medicaid for nursing homes and home health care indicate the cost to Medicare was $1.6 billion, while the same programs cost Medicaid $13.8 billion. At the same time it became increasingly recognized that many people were in nursing homes, reimbursed by Medicaid, because there were no health and social supports available to maintain them in their own homes and communities. Therefore thirty-five states in 1983 requested and received the new home- and community-based waiver program designed as an alternative to nursing home care. Major rationales for requesting the waivers were to prevent premature institutionalization of older people who preferred to stay at home and to reduce the Medicaid cost of nursing homes (Zawadski 1984: 16; Pallay & Oktay 1983: 3, 8).

In one state the Medicaid-covered services under the waiver provision appropriate for older people include the following: Community care services for those people who qualify for nursing home services, but who are able to reside in their homes or communities with the aid of home-delivered meals, alternative living, adult day rehabilitation, respite care, homemaker aide, or emergency response system services (which secures appropriate services from existing public and private providers wherever possible).

According to the Georgia *Medicaid Guide* (pp. 6–8), some of the provisions which apply to older people are:

1. Mental health clinic services for emotionally or mentally disturbed individuals, drug or alcohol abusers, and mentally retarded or developmentally disabled persons

2. Nonemergency transportation to obtain medical treatment or health-related services

3. Nursing home services for those needing intermediate or skilled nursing care prescribed by a physician

4. Eyeglasses needed as a result of cataract surgery, enucleation, or retinitis pigmentosa

5. Artificial limbs, braces, hearing aids, and such which assist or replace bodily functions

6. A limited number of prescribed drugs and supplies on a monthly basis

7. A limited number of physician visits for diagnosis and treatment

8. Diagnosis and treatment of foot ailments by podiatrists

9. Diagnosis and treatment of personality and mental disorders, by psychologists with a limited number of treatment hours

10. Rural health clinic services are covered for medical services and supplies.

As a point of reference, the 1988 Rivlin and Wiener study found that in 1985 there were 28.6 million Americans over age 65, of whom 6.3 million were disabled. One and a third million lived in nursing homes, and 4.9 million lived in the community (table 1-1), where they are cared for by family and friends, sometimes supplemented by paid services. The projection of disabled elderly into the twenty-first century is for a tremendous increase, as greater numbers of people live into their eighties and nineties. Even with much more community care, which prevents premature institutionalization, there also will be more older people who require nursing home care. Thus, the need for nursing homes will not diminish over time. How will public health insurance collect, handle, and pay for an ever-increasing number of people needing all types of health care?

CHAPTER 4

Motor Disability

Lack of mobility in the elderly is a serious disability. Devices such as canes and crutches have been in use for over two thousand years. Today, rehabilitative technology has developed highly specialized forms of aids such as: user-controlled wheelchairs, collapsible wheelchairs which can be transported, battery-powered individual vehicles, walkers, specialized canes and crutches, and splints and braces adapted for specific conditions. In addition to such mechanical help, medications and high-technology interventions also contribute to the diminution of motor disability.

The causes for motor disability range from birth anomalies to accidents and trauma which can occur at any age and affect many parts of the body. Some chronic diseases and hysterical paralytic reactions due to psychiatric causes as well as to a variety of neuromuscular disorders also can affect motor ability. This chapter is limited to mobility problems due to arthritis and to cerebrovascular accidents (CVA) that occur primarily as people age.

Berkow (1982: 770) points out that in 1940 there were two main categories of the most common types of arthritis: rheumatoid arthritis (RA) and osteoarthritis (OA). In 1982 there were over one hundred specifically identifiable conditions of the rheumatic diseases.

The etiology of rheumatoid arthritis is unknown, but when present it is a chronic syndrome characterized by nonspecific, usually symmetric inflammation of the peripheral joints, potentially resulting in progressive destruction of articular and periarticular structures. . . . It is possible that adult RA may occur suddenly with simultaneous inflammation in multiple joints. However, it more frequently develops insidiously with progressive joint involvement. Tenderness and eventual swelling of the affected joints are the most observable symptoms and signs along with stiffness of 30 minutes duration on arising in the morning and after prolonged inactivity. Deformities may develop rapidly, particularly flexion contractures. (Berkow 1982: 779)

Osteoarthritis (OA) is the most common form of arthritis among older people. In essence it develops when cartilage repair does not keep pace with cartilage degeneration. It also may develop secondary to other diseases. Both forms of arthritis are characterized by joint inflammation and much pain—often intense and, in the case of RA, with possible progressive deformity of the affected parts. The specific causes of RA and OA are unknown but may be influenced by many internal factors. In people over age forty they occur more frequently in women than in men (Berkow 1982: 793).

When the development of arthritis is slow and insidious, personality and behavioral changes occur gradually over time. The affected individual usually seeks medical attention only after the symptoms become too uncomfortable to perform the usual activities of daily living (ADL). Treatment of the symptoms usually involves changes in the person's routine: pain-relieving medication, rest periods, passive and active exercise therapy, a healthful diet, and follow-up medical visits to monitor effects of medication and other routines (Arthritis Foundation 1984). These obviously affect the daily routine and social functioning.

Johnston (1984) points out that psychological changes which occur may be reactions to the loss of functional ability or may be symptomatic of the disease (such as occurs in Alzheimer's). Another important factor affecting the individual's reaction to arthritis is influenced by the unpredictability of the progressive disease, which may have periods of remission. The lack of personal control over its overall progression can lead to anger, anxiety, and depression. "Learned helplessness" and increased, possibly exacerbated, dependency on others are frequent reactions. Most people react according to their total life history and development, and to the extrinsic factors of family, employers, and others to them and to the disease (Johnston 1984: 41; Kerson & Kerson 1985: 28, 31–34).

On the other hand, onset of a cerebrovascular accident (CVA), or stroke, which also can affect mobility, is precipitous. The cerebral insufficiency due to a transient disturbance of blood flow to the brain, if of short duration, usually permits brain tissue recovery and the symptoms disappear. If, however, there is cerebral infarction, the results are often catastrophic. Most cerebrovascular illnesses are secondary to atherosclerotic disease, hypertension, or a combination of both. Symptoms and signs reflect the area of the brain that is damaged and not necessarily the artery that is affected. The completed stroke is clinically manifested by neurologic deficits of varying severity. The first few days after the abrupt onset are crucial, due to the possibility of cerebral edema or, less frequently, to extension of the infarct. The specific neurologic symptoms are determined by the site of the brain infarct, and any part of the body, including the senses as well as bodily organs, can be affected in a variety of combinations (Berkow 1982: 875).

EFFECTS ON THE INDIVIDUAL AND FAMILY

People with either RA or OA need to, and usually do, learn their own parameters and pace their activities accordingly. Pain and fatigue often are constant companions to arthritic disease. Uncertainty about periods of remission, exacerbation and progression of the disease add to the struggle needed to avoid isolation, anxiety, and depression. Families and care givers need to learn to handle their own anxieties and to be sensitive to the physical and psychological needs of the arthritic sufferer (Kerson & Kerson 1985: 30).

The sequelae of a stroke, which may include limited mobility, also tend to involve other parts of the body. Hemiplegia, speech, hearing, memory, and/or dexterity loss, and some cognition disturbance may be involved. The functional parameters of the person after a CVA may require changes in ADL care housing, life-style, and social activities. The process of rehabilitation is arduous and slow, requiring sustained determination to reach the maximum level of functioning. Care givers and family members need to work toward understanding the problems, to develop greater patience with the patient's slow progress, and they often require sustained support to do so.

One example, from the closed records of a home health agency, involves a seven-person family living in a very crowded second-floor apartment. The patient, Mrs. S., had her own room. She had two years of schooling and previously performed domestic work. The home situation was considered poor. Mrs. S.'s son worked, his wife was pregnant with a fifth child, there was no phone, and there were family arguments while the nurse was present.

Mrs. S. was referred to the home health agency by a medical social worker because she did not keep medical appointments at the clinic. The presenting problem was hemiplegia/unspecified, causing her to be bedridden. Other diagnoses included an acute, ill-defined CVA disease in 1984, fracture of tarsal and metatarsal bones in 1985, and a urinary tract infection, site not specified, in 1986. Also, it was noted that many teeth were missing and there was some question about whether or not the patient was mentally retarded. The notes indicated Mrs. S. needed to learn to handle transfers and ADL, and needed supervision with ambulation. The notes cautioned she should not be left alone or unattended. The patient indicated she did not like help from household members.

There were two different case managers sequentially involved, with some differences of approach or attitude. One indicated the need to assess the patient's condition for physical/mental limitations to self-care, the need for adaptive equipment and assistance to secure it, and the need for acceptance of the loss of independence. This case manager also suggested referrals to appropriate community resources, such as homemaker/home health aide for assistance with personal care and to teach self-care within physical/mental limitations, teach use of appropriate community resources and teach an emergency plan.

The second case manager listed goals, stating, "The patient will . . ." with dates for each goal and intervention, and assessment of each intervention. In addition this case manager suggested it was important to promote a listening atmosphere to allow ventilation of feelings and allow the patient to express concern about changes in her life-style. She also wanted the family and patient taught to report any significant changes to the health care team and to have and understand an emergency plan. Her comments indicated the patient was oriented and cooperative but depressed. She added that her oral functioning was adequate for eating, but speech was generally unintelligible except for social speech (automatic "hi," etc.) with expressive aphasia and apraxia.

Mrs. S. said the family would help with bathing and bed changes. She did not want a home health aide to assist with personal care. The family refused to permit any speech therapy, which was ordered.

After one and a half months of the home health agency's active participation, the patient's physical condition appeared to deteriorate. At that point she was discharged because the nurse and staff had been menacingly approached by three men in the neighborhood on their way to a home visit. On the last visit they promised to talk with the referring case worker about a transfer to a high-rise setting where there could be more use of the wheelchair. If this happened the agency would continue with her.

Home health agencies are reimbursed by public or private insurance for their visits and treatment only when the patients are homebound and when ordered by a physician as medically necessary. Generally home health agencies need to focus on the physical aspects of the patient's disease and progress. Many records indicate some awareness of other social and/or emotional needs of the patient, rarely those of the care-giving family. The records also indicate some awareness of the need for and use of community resources other than the home health agency itself. However, in the example used as well as in many other records pursued, there is no documentation of referrals actually made. It is possible they may have been made but not recorded, because they were not considered germane to the physical health of the patient.

Home health agencies clearly delineate the functions of registered nurses and health aides, but the functions of case managers, besides observing needs, are not clear from the records read by this author. The prime focus of home health agencies must be on the physical health of the patient and help to the care-giving families to learn to care properly for the patient. It also is true that heavy caseloads, strict limitations of both public and private health insurance reimbursements, and detailed medical recording requirements for each visit put a great deal of pressure on staffs of home health agencies. However, case managers are expected to explore, and utilize, community resources, which can help to mitigate some of the pressures and problems of patients and their families so that the health needs can be more comprehensively addressed and, hopefully, ameliorated.

Specifically, Mrs. S., living in very crowded conditions with unwilling care givers, was referred due to missed medical appointments. She needed a panoply of community resources. Some of the most obvious included transportation to enable her to keep medical appointments and to have a dental clinic evaluate her (which is important for nutritional needs, self-esteem, and basic communication). After dental needs are met, mental ability can be better evaluated. The record did not indicate whether any professional worker involved with this patient had made such referrals. The needs of the family as a whole appeared not addressed. When the home health agency staff noted the deterioration of the patient, before they were accosted on the street, why didn't this staff request further medical evaluation?

The second example is an eighty-seven-year-old woman who had suffered a CVA. The material for this was taken from both the chart for her social history and a family conference held at the rehabilitation center where she was undergoing treatment.

Mrs. M. has two sons and one daughter. One son has "expressive difficulty," the other children, both married, lived in another state. Mrs. M. enjoyed "doing for others." She had been a college dormitory mother and after retirement chauffeured friends to church and on their errands. She also was a sunday school teacher and active in her church. She suffered a left hemisphere CVA, leaving her with right-sided hemiparesis.

The family conference included Mrs. M., the son with his wife who lived in another state, and the total rehabilitation team. Each member of the team reported the gains Mrs. M. made during her stay, pointing out she had achieved from 70 to 80 percent independence in many ADL tasks. Very recently, Mrs. M. became able to chew some solid food; and "only yesterday" took her first step unaided. However, each specialist emphasized the continuing need for patience by both professional and family care givers, and the need for frequent hints, clues, and encouragement to help Mrs. M. remember what she has relearned. They each stressed the need for patience and continuing therapy after discharge. In particular, the physician emphasized it might take approximately a year before Mrs. M.'s full capacity is known and reached.

The son raised specific issues, such as walking independently, eating in a restaurant, independent toileting, driving to another state where Mrs. M. will live with her daughter, and independent dressing and grooming. The staff indicated a brace was needed to sustain the weak leg and should be used; a wheelchair was imperative for walking distances and for long outings. The social worker suggested the family take Mrs. M. for an outing later that day and then come back with more questions.

During her remaining two-week stay at the rehabilitation center, Mrs. M. will be taken on many outings to help accustom her to ordinary community facilities. She will receive a thorough physical checkup before discharge. Discharge planning includes review of the equipment and assistive devices that are needed. The daughter-in-law requested a copy of the tape of the interview (recorded for this work) for the daughter in whose home Mrs. M. will live. She thought it would be helpful to hear of Mrs. M.'s slow progress and the concerns and caring of the staff. This was provided for the family.

The family conference indicates a comprehensive approach and integrated focus by the rehabilitation staff. It also indicates that family members need much more help than only one meeting to understand how to live with the sequelae and deficits of a CVA. The patient also needs more help to accept the limitations of her current situation. Mrs. M.'s clearly stated desired goal, to drive others to church, unrealistic though it is, may be the impetus that drives her to strive for as much physical independence as possible. Questions from the son clearly indicate his hope for future complete physical independence for his mother and his lack of real comprehension of her limited condition. The staff stressed patience and gentle encouragement throughout the conference. It is hoped that either the social worker or the psychologist will meet with family members to suggest that they might find psychotherapeutic support helpful after returning home, to help them adjust to their mother's more limited abilities. It would be helpful to Mrs. M. if, after regaining more skills, some way could be found for her to help others, since this was the pattern of her life-style.

A study of discharge from an acute care hospital to the community (Castillo & Hall 1987) points up the need for careful planning to help patients with mobility problems. The authors point out that written home care instructions are a major asset for adherence to the continuity of quality care. (308–310). Written instructions act as reminders, standards, and goals for both the patient and the care givers. Whenever people are stressed or when the life situation has changed, it is helpful to have something tangible and concrete to hold onto for support or reference, whether it is a care plan, a schedule, guidelines, or a list of available resources.

ACTIVITIES OF SOCIAL FUNCTIONING

The examples in the previous section, by implication, outline the lack of social functioning when people are homebound, even when there is family to help them. Social activities were not overtly considered by the home health agency and were barely considered by the rehabilitation center.

The example for this section, of a less disabled person, clearly indicates the importance of social functioning. Material was gathered from social agency records, an individual interview, and a group interview in a group home for older people. Mrs. B. is eighty-eight years old and very heavy, with arthritis in both knees. Additionally, she has Type II diabetes and takes heart and ulcer medications. Her neurologic examination was normal, with no diabetic neuropathy. She uses an ordinary cane to aid mobility, although a four-prong cane was recommended.

Mrs. B. is one of eight children born in Europe, probably in Poland. She is a Holocaust survivor who witnessed atrocities, including the murder of her father. Five of her siblings survived in the United States, and some are living in other cities. Mrs. B. has one daughter living in the same city, who is her informal care giver and devoted to her.

Mrs. B. is a widow who lived in a senior citizen subsidized apartment. She was able to get from there to the community center for companionship and a full meal five days weekly. When her arthritis progressed to the point that precluded her living alone, she moved to her employed daughter's apartment. The daughter needed to continue working, which left Mrs. B. completely dependent on her to leave the apartment for all excursions including attendance at the community center. The daughter arranged with a neighbor to look in on her mother periodically. This arrangement put pressure on both the mother and daughter, which was destroying their good relationship. When an opportunity arose to move into a group home with eight other residents and a chair lift to get up and down the stairs, she reluctantly moved there.

In an interview, Mrs. B. indicated she hated to give up going to the community center, but had looked forward to being with her daughter. She was very ambivalent about staying with her daughter. She wanted to be with her, but "didn't want to be on her head." Mrs. B. stated she missed her former friends and activities at the community center. When moving from her daughter's apartment to the group home, Mrs. B. felt she was being pushed out and cried a great deal both before and after this move. However, the friendly atmosphere and companionship of the other residents—plus her daughter's continued interest, which included frequent visits and outings together—helped to assuage her feelings of hurt and abandonment.

In the group interview with all the residents, Mrs. B. said this was much better than living all alone. Crocheting, taking care of children, and helping others had been enjoyable activities, but had become too difficult. She likes to read and watch television, but newspaper print is too small for her. She enjoys the visits from children and adults to the group home. There is a van available to take residents on a variety of small trips to parks, theaters, the beauty parlor, and so on, but Mrs. B. cannot use this due to difficulty entering and leaving the van. She relies on her daughter to take her on such outings. This is satisfactory for both of them. Mrs. B. stayed at the group home for four years before her arthritis worsened, causing many falls, which necessitated her moving to a more protected setting.

It is clear that socializing and focusing outside of herself was very important to Mrs. B.'s quality of life and helped preserve her functioning. The staff at the group home verbally indicated it was sheer will power that kept her active and participating as long as she did. The needs of the daughter were balanced better with her mother's when they lived apart.

These three very different examples indicate how housing, the family, and social atmosphere in which a person lives, affects the functioning and attitudes of those with mobility limitations.

The last example touched on the effects of lack of mobility on the person, on the family and home setting, and on activities of social functioning. It is almost impossible to isolate these factors from the physical problem of lack of mobility. Activities of social functioning are considered very important in helping arthritis victims reduce isolation and depression (Kerson & Kerson 1985: 27–28). This is equally true for those with other chronic disabilities that hinder social interaction.

ORGANIZATION OR INSTITUTION INVOLVEMENT

The material for this example came from an interview with the administrator of the Center for Rehabilitation Medicine on March 22, 1988, and a brochure celebrating the tenth anniversary of the center. In this instance, the concern and outreach of professionals resulted in the development of a new institution to help those with mobility and other limitations.

A small rehabilitation program was begun in 1945 at a medical school teaching hospital due to the stimulation of one physician. This program started the development of services and training, with the assistance of the State Division of Vocational Rehabilitation to create the Emory University Regional and Training Center in a public hospital, which continued without major changes until 1965. At that time the university created the Department of Physical Medicine and Rehabilitation, permitting enlargement of the small program. The following year a twenty-two-bed ward of physical medicine and rehabilitation was opened at the public hospital.

During 1970 the university received a grant from a local foundation to conduct a study of its program and facility needs on the campus. The Department of Physical Medicine and Rehabilitation was included in this study. Four years later plans were approved and funding allocated for construction of a six-floor facility with fifty-six inpatient beds and large areas for outpatient care, training activities, and rehabilitative research. In 1976 the first outpatients were treated. Also in that year the Departments of Physical Therapy and Rehabilitation Nursing were established. The following year the first inpatients were admitted, although the bed capacity at that time was only twenty-four, and other departments were added. These included Occupational Therapy, Social Service, Dietetics, Vocational Rehabilitation, and Communication Disorders.

Gradually other specialties were added until, by 1987, the center included the following departments: Communication Disorders with eight full-time therapists; Dietetics with sixteen professionals provid-

ing almost three hundred meals daily plus in-depth nutritional assessments and care plans for each patient; Occupational Therapy with
many different innovative programs such as biofeedback, FES, a patient computer for cognitive retraining, stress management, pet therapy, project magic, regular patient outings, and adapted sports;
Physical Therapy with fifteen therapists and nine aides was used both
for in- and outpatients; Psychology with both neuropsychologists and
clinical psychologists provided individual, group, and family therapy
plus teaching and research; and Social Service with a supervisor, three
staff social workers, and one assistant to do the psychosocial histories
on admission and be professionally active. Physicians and nurses were
not listed as separate departments.

Representatives of all departments who have contact with a patient
are involved in periodic team planning and in discharge planning with
the patient and the family.

Over the years other developments have included accreditation
from the Commission of Rehabilitation Facilities and a computerized
data bank for program evaluation. A Regional Research and Training
Center grant was awarded for the study of head injury and stroke.
The Health Enhancement Program was expanded to include early
phases of cardiac rehabilitation. The outpatient clinics also have expanded to include specialists in muscular dystrophy, head injury, or-
thotics and prosthetics, electromyography, physical medicine, cardiac
rehabilitation, hemophilia, arthritis, and pediatrics.

All inpatients need to be referred by physicians, although the outpatient clinics are open to the entire community. The majority are
referred locally or statewide, although there are some from the southeastern United States and a few from foreign countries.

The administrator pointed out that the average age of inpatients is
the mid-fifties. In one quarter, out of eighty inpatients, thirty-four
were over age sixty-five. The older patients are admitted primarily for
strokes with hemiplegia and for accidents or falls. The administrator
felt the older patient is less responsive to therapy because deficits
tend to become permanent. The facility has no private rooms, and
sixteen beds are reserved for head injuries. The last two factors affect
the size of the waiting list. The waiting period is approximately two
weeks.

The administrator said that despite all the equipment necessary for
rehabilitation, this specialty is more labor-intensive than capital-

intensive. The center is exempt from the diagnostic related group (DRG) guidelines for length of patient stay. Income is derived from patient out-of-pocket funds, private health insurance, and both Medicaid and Medicare reimbursement.

Now that the center is fully established, it is working on a full affiliation with the city's only geriatric hospital which will include a two-way flow of patients as well as consultations between the staffs. The hospital underwrites the center, which has had financial losses since its inception.

In 1987 the center joined the newly formed Georgia Consortium on the Psychology of Aging. The consortium consists of the Emory University School of Medicine, Departments of Psychiatry and Rehabilitation Medicine; the Georgia Institute of Technology, School of Psychology; the Medical College of Georgia; Veterans Administration medical centers in two cities; and the University of Georgia Gerontology Center. The purpose of this consortium is to share training, education, and research resources with the specific aim of providing the highest possible quality of pre- and postdoctoral training in the psychology of aging. The consortium is a vehicle in which psychologists and other behavioral scientists can interact on a regular basis. Cooperative arrangements have been made so that expertise from member institutions can be used to supplement existing training programs. (All the material on the consortium is from a brochure made available at the 1990 annual meeting of the Georgia Gerontology Society in Athens, Georgia). This is considered significant as one example of the new emphasis on interdisciplinary training in higher education. Hopefully it will lead to increased interdisciplinary functioning with patients, clients, and their families and with policy-setting individuals in government.

The aspects of the Center for Rehabilitation Medicine that indicate professional health care providers reaching beyond the parameters of their job functions were the beliefs and convictions of those early physical medicine physicians who worked and pushed for the establishment of rehabilitation activities. Originally these focused primarily on vocational rehabilitation. Some might label this type of expansion as the beginning of "empire building." However, it did provide a service needed by the community. As the center grew, the concept of rehabilitative services for all ages developed, and as research and training grants were secured for head injury and stroke, older people beyond the usual age of employment were included. Participation in the Consortium on the Psychology of Aging certainly is beyond the parameters of usual job functions of rehabilitation specialists. This might be considered an incremental development among specialists who habitually function within an interdisciplinary setting for the total rehabilitation of the patient. This example indicates one way professional outreach can lead to area-wide institutional development.

GOVERNMENT INVOLVEMENT

Government sections in previous chapters have not focused on federal financial involvement. But before examining federal financial commitments, it should be noted that state and local governments sponsor some public accommodations for those of all ages with mobility limitations, such as "kneeling" buses and dips in sidewalk crossing areas. All government buildings now are required to be accessible to the handicapped for egress and in toileting facilities. The newer municipal rapid transit lines also have similar accommodations. Many department stores, office buildings, and other facilities serving the public have adapted older buildings to these new regulations. In these ways government is helpful to those with mobility disability.

Mention also must be made of government-sponsored rehabilitation centers. The Roosevelt Warm Springs Institute for Rehabilitation is an example of one which includes services for older people. This comprehensive center includes careful discharge planning and return to the community.

Burns (1971) noted that government support for research in health fields increased from $72.9 million in fiscal 1950 to $1.69 billion in fiscal 1970. Only $73 million in 1970 came from outside the federal government. Some of the research is undertaken by the federal government through various divisions of the Public Health Service, such as the National Institutes of Health (NIH), the National Center for Health Services and Development, and the National Center for Health Statistics. Much federally supported research takes the form of grants and research contracts to state and local agencies, private institutions, universities, and hospitals outside the government. Other components of the Department of Health Education and Welfare (now called the Department of Health and Human Services [DHHS]), such as the Social Security Administration and the Children's Bureau, also administer research funds (p. 512). The Administration on Aging (AoA) supports education, training, demonstration, and research grants.

Grants provided by the NIH and the AoA are the examples of federal government involvement considered in this chapter. Initially, under the direction of other health institutes, the first aging research under the NIH was started in 1940. In 1974 Public Law 93-296 authorized the establishment of the National Institute of Aging (NIA), which required the new institute to develop a comprehensive national plan for research on aging in cooperation with other DHEW agencies involved in such research. In 1975 the National Advisory Council on Aging was organized and the Gerontology Research Center and the Adult Development and Aging Branch separated from their parent institute to become the core of the NIA. (National Institute on Aging, Information Office 1983: 5).

This institute (NIA) was authorized for the "conduct and support of biomedical, social and behavioral research and training related to the aging process and the diseases and other special problems and needs of the aged." Wording of the 1975 act declared, "the study of the aging process, the one biological condition common to all, has not received research support commensurate with its effects on the lives of every individual," and pointed out that "recent research efforts point the way toward alleviation of the problems of old age by extending the healthy middle years of life" (NIA Information Office 1983: 4).

By 1988 the NIA consisted of two intramural and three extramural programs. The intramural programs include:

1. The Gerontology Research Center for research on the basic mechanisms of aging, started in 1958, which now includes women as well as men

2. The Epidemiology, Demography, and Biometry program which conducts and supports research in the epidemiology of health and disease, and the demographic, social, and economic factors that affect the health status of older people

The extramural programs include:

1. The Biomedical Research and Clinical Medicine programs which fund research on immunology, genetics, molecular

and cellular biology, exercise, physiology, nutrition, endocrinology and geriatric medicine, and facilities that provide resources needed in aging research projects

2. The Behavioral and Social Research program which supports research and training on social and behavioral factors that affect the process of growing old and the place of older people in society, especially as they interact with biomedical processes influencing health and effective functioning as people age

3. The Neuroscience and Neuropsychology of Aging programs which foster and support extramural and collaborative research and training on the aging process relevant to the neurosciences and associated area of psychological sciences

There is a newly established Office of Planning, Analysis and Communication that includes the Public Information Office, which provides the mandated education program for the general public, mass media, other government agencies, and service organizations.

The NIA Special Report on Aging (Administrative Document, June 1988: 3) highlights research conducted by the NIA and other NIH institutes. The highest research priorities of the NIA at that time included Alzheimer's disease; improved understanding of the basic mechanisms and characteristics of aging; hip fractures focusing on osteoporosis, falls, and gait disturbances; strategies for promoting health and effective functioning in older people; and training and career development in geriatrics and aging research.

There are two types of research grants. One needs to be multidisciplinary with three or more individual projects. The other provides ten types of awards, which specify requirements for the applicants and may be allotted to individuals, medical schools, teaching nursing homes, pilot projects, and universities (NIA 1983: 3–5).

The booklet *Research Advances in Aging 1984–1986* (NIA 1987: 1, 19, 25, 29, 30) discusses the progress and findings of thirty-eight research projects supported by the NIA. Two focused on hip fractures and two on bone loss in aging, which can impede mobility as can arthritis and CVAs. Many of the other studies related to basic factors in cellular and physiological aspects of aging as well as to behaviors influencing the health of older people. Eight of the thirty-eight related to memory loss and dementias, one to hearing loss. The rest were widely scattered. Other NIH–sponsored research on the problems of aging during 1987 involved the National Cancer Institute; the National Heart, Lung and Blood Institute; the National Institute of Neurological and Communicative Disorders and Stroke; the National Institute of Allergy and Infectious Diseases; and the National Eye Institute. The Division of Research Resources also has ongoing research of benefit to older people. Other NIH institutes supporting research on aging include the NI of Diabetes and Digestive and Kidney Diseases; and the NI of Arthritis and Musculoskeletal and Skin Diseases.

Of the 215 NIH grants and contracts active on December 1, 1987, 181 were provided to universities and colleges, 20 went to private corporations or organizations, 8 went to other federal agencies, and 6 to medical centers, including Veterans Administration facilities. The titles revealed 13 focused on cognition in later life, 3 on mental health, 2 related to hearing problems, 3 related to mobility problems, and 6 to interdisciplinary training. Thus 27 related to problems of interest in this work. It is possible that studies which focused on other aspects of aging, such as nutrition, care givers and support networks, and epidemiology, probably also related in some fashion to the disabilities here (NILIA ADRES-Report Act 100 BSR Active and Obligated Grants and Contracts, 12-1-1987).

The Administration on Aging (AoA) compendium of active grants (January 1988) provides somewhat more information. The AoA awarded 268 grants in FY 1987 for demonstration, education, training, and research. Technical assistance is considered a different category. One of the latter went to a private organization, 3 went to federal agencies, and 2 to medical centers. Organizations receiving the remaining grants included private corporations or organizations, 1; professional organizations 10; social or health agencies serving the elderly, 15; individual state agencies or subdivisions thereof, 38; and colleges and universities, 184.

A very gross breakdown by major focus of each grant is revealing. Forty-four grants were for continuing education and training of professionals and paraprofessionals. Related to that were 8 more for development of academic institutions, faculty, and/or curricula. Thirty-four grants related to community-based care systems, their development, improvement, and linkages. There were 24 grants related to informal care giving. Health promotion and health education were next with 21, legal services related to the elderly had 18 grants, both preparation for aging and supportive services each received 15. Twelve grants were given for career preparation for professionals and/ or paraprofessionals, compared to almost four times that number for continuing education and training. Alzheimer's disease, elder abuse, and placement and internship programs each received 10 grants. Twenty-three grants of the 268 clearly related to problems of interest to this work, although some of the others also may have impinged on these disabilities.

Despite the focus as expressed in the titles, there must have been overlapping. For example, 10 grants were awarded to Alzheimer's disease, but informal care giving with 24, community-based care systems with 34, and supportive services with 15 all may be related to Alzheimer's disease as well.

Did the number of grants awarded relate primarily to needs of the elderly as perceived by the AoA and by the organizations applying for them or did they relate more to the "grantsmanship" skills and historical focus of the applicants? The large number of grants given for education, continuing education, and training may indicate there is a great need to educate faculty members about the process of healthy aging and problems associated with it. It may be that only in the 1980s did many colleges and universities begin to work with other professions such as health care and social service as collaborators, although educators were working with other disciplines within the field of education (from abstracts from the Association for Gerontology in Higher Education annual meeting, 1989). The historical approach of educators had been within their own academic disciplines, which tended to limit concepts of innovative demonstration programs and innovative research in collaboration with other disciplines not in academia.

The NIA mission stated in Public Law 93-296 (NIA Information Office 1983: 5) was to "develop a comprehensive national plan for research on aging in cooperation with other agencies." In all the material shared with this author by both the NIA and the AoA there was no other mention of a comprehensive national plan. The grants and awards of each agency seem to indicate their individual foci and major interests.

The attention of both the NIA and the AoA may change slightly with the 1991 passage of the Americans with Disabilities Act, although some experts in both fields (disabilities and aging) indicate

> different priorities and attitudes and competition for scarce resources have made coalitions between the aging and people with disabilities tenuous and, at times, difficult to maintain. Still, common ground between aging and disabled populations is vast and opportunities for cooperation remain great. . . . There are differences in the outlooks of younger and older people with disabilities, but we haven't really sat down with groups long enough to see what they are. (Lederer 1991: 1–3)

The high proportion of research grants from both the NIA and the AoA going to colleges and universities raises a number of concerns which cannot be addressed in this work. The most obvious relate to the possibility of unnecessary duplication of resources and effort. Are there categories of colleges and universities and groups of elderly that appear not to receive grants? Why? Does any knowledgeable body address these questions?

The NIA and other NIHs involved with aging, the AoA, particularly through Titles III and IV, and the panoply of congressional committees having "jurisdiction over major program areas relating to the elderly" provide a smorgasbord of " 'incomprehensible' administrative organization of services for the elderly" (Rich and Baum 1984: 10–11). The Americans with Disabilities Act adds yet another component to this mélange.

Perhaps the time has come to consider a convocation of all federal government organizations, agencies, institutes, and congressional committees concerned with all aspects of healthy, disabled, and diseased aging. The prime purpose of such a meeting might be to consider a national unified plan of services to, research about, responsibility for, and the authority to carry out all federal activity related to aging. Hopefully, all the knowledge, scientific advances, and experience gathered to date might influence the outcome. This might become a comprehensive plan, which might allot all available monies for direct service, research, education, training, demonstration projects, and future planning.

HEALTH INSURANCE: HEALTH MAINTENANCE ORGANIZATIONS

Public insurance for the financially needy of all ages and for those over age sixty-five is very uneven for the chronically mobility disabled. Reimbursements are provided on an outpatient basis only when "medically necessary" as ordered by the physician and administered by Medicare-certified specialists until the patient reaches a stable level. Medicare does reimburse for durable medical equipment such as wheelchairs, crutches, artificial limbs, and prosthetic devices, and artificial internal organs. A limited amount of home care, which includes skilled nursing, physical therapy, home health aid, limited social services, and other therapies through certified home health agencies, can be reimbursed only when the physician indicates this is medically necessary while the patient is homebound and can demonstrate improvement (*The Medicare Handbook* 1990: 9).

It should be obvious that the chronically disabled have chronic health care expenses both in and out of hospitals and need insurance that provides this varied and intermittent form of coverage over a period of years. Medicaid provides more help in such cases than does any other form of general health insurance, as of this writing. It is not known what provisions private insurance long-term-care policies make for those older people with mobility disability beyond the usual 20 percent of Medicare-approved coverage.

Group practice was initiated by some physicians as early as 1946 (Pechansky et al. 1968: 182) and has grown tremendously since then. Health maintenance organizations (HMOs), as we know them today, started during World War II. The Kaiser shipbuilding company on the West Coast, concerned about absenteeism among its workers, which was hampering the war effort, initiated the Kaiser Plan, which spread to other war-related industries.

HMOs differ from traditional fee-for-service payment for health care, for both in- and outpatient care. They require a large number of subscribers whose fees are prepaid, and physicians, nurses, ancillary services, and support staff to cover the health needs of enrollees. Specialist medical staff and other health care specialists may be part-time or full-time employees of the HMO. Enrollees are required to select personal physicians from the HMO panel, and physicians are required to accept the annual salary set by the HMO. Thus, an HMO incorporates both the health care services rendered and a method of payment for them (Myers 1971: 2–3).

These concepts were actively opposed by the established medical community. A serious problem for the early HMOs was securing hospital privileges for their physicians (Safford 1968: 219). Some of the early well-known prepaid health plans which weathered the intense opposition of the AMA included the Kaiser Foundation Health Plan, the United Mine Workers of America Welfare and Retirement Fund, the Group Health Cooperative of Puget Sound in Seattle, Group Health Association in Washington, DC, and the Health Insurance Plan of Greater New York (Safford 1968: 219; Brindle 1969: 37–38). Many factors in the 1960s pushed for acceptance of HMOs. These included disenchantment with the "experts" and the growing concept of self-help (Naisbitt 1982: 134; Leyerle 1984: 24; Ginzberg 1985: 162), the spiraling costs of health care to the government and to employers (Califano 1986: 4), as well as the continued record of the early ongoing, nonprofit HMOs of lesser and shorter hospitalizations by their enrollees (Department of Health Education and Welfare, 1973: 6–7).

The federal administration offered "prepaid and organized comprehensive health care systems servicing defined populations," more commonly known as HMOs, to offset the fragmentation, unequal geographical resources, and ever-increasing costs in health care. The federal guidelines spelled out by Beverlee Myers, assistant administrator for Resource Development, Health Services and Mental Health Administration, included the following objectives: provide a choice as to the health care system they may use; attempt to reform the health care delivery system; include incentives for cost control by the delivery system itself; improve the ability of federal and state programs to control their expenditures with predictable prepaid contracts for beneficiaries; provide incentives for health maintenance rather than crisis-oriented medical care; and use HMOs as a mechanism to correct the maldistribution of health services. Allocation of federal support is based on the rationale that the entire population should have the HMO alternative. The HMO represents a reorganization of those health services that already exist; it is not designed to create new services (Myers 1971: 1).

Myers explained that an HMO is an arrangement between four essential elements: an organized delivery system, including manpower

and facilities to provide or arrange for all health services for the enrolled population; an enrolled population who contract for a range of
health services for which the system assumes responsibility; a financial
plan that underwrites the costs of agreed-upon services on a prene-
gotiated and prepaid basis; and a managing organization that assures
legal, fiscal, public, and professional accountability. Myers pointed out
that any "one element may assume the corporate focal point for organizing and managing an HMO" (Myers 1971: 2). In some instances
managing organizations have developed "managed care services"
which may be but are not necessarily HMOs. Myers indicated the
enrollment figures of HMOs are important to the government as a
means of predicting costs. She provided the governmental financial
guidelines involved in starting an HMO and specified guidelines for
all sponsoring management groups (Myers 1971: 4–6). It appears that
the president's proposal allowed and encouraged enough options as
to offer a "smorgasbord" that included profit-making sponsors, and
alleviated legal barriers to formation of some types of HMOs which
had been set up in some states.

In 1973 legislation passed by Congress provided the go-ahead for
the federal government to support the development of HMOs, independent practice associations (IPAs) by physicians or medical societies, private for-profit insurance companies, and consumer-controlled
groups (Roemer 1982: 40). It was in the early 1980s

> when many employers got behind them and encouraged their
> workers to sign up. . . . Little attention has been given to the
> fact that most of the new HMOs were developed by for-profit
> organizations that did not conform to the classic staff model,
> but relied instead on individual or IPAs. More important, the
> new Federal guidelines tightening admissions and length of stay
> in acute-care hospitals reduces . . . the principal competitive ad-
> vantage of HMOs over fee-for-service medicine. (Ginzberg
> 1988: 3648)

In an effort to discover to what degree the HMOs in Georgia
served people over age sixty-five and which services they provided to
older people with disabilities of interest to this work, all HMOs licensed by the Commissioner of Insurance's office were reached by
letter with telephone follow-up in 1989. The letter requested re-

sponses from each HMO on their sponsorship and coverage for enrollees over age 65. Unless otherwise stated, the responses were
secured by telephone, from the ten licensed HMOs. Five were not
functional for the following reasons: one was going through the process of either being sold or closing operations; another said it was not
active in the HMO business; one refused to participate in any way;
another said it could not participate for a long time; the fifth, an
interstate company, said its office here had been closed for almost
three years.

The other five HMOs listed were active in the state. Only one was
active outside the metropolitan area of the capital city. It is locally
owned and operated. That one, I was told, has no Medicare supplement. An enrolled employee with a dependent over age sixty-five is
referred to some other health resource in the area.

One HMO is part of a national insurance company which organized
it for profits. Subscribers over age sixty-five and their families are
eligible if employed and can convert to individual policies on retirement. This plan does not provide individual health screenings. It is a
"federally qualified HMO." However, this plan does include treatment for problems of cognition, hearing, and mobility, if such treatment is considered "medically necessary." Cataracts are covered in
this plan, but hearing aids are not, because the latter are not considered to be "technically medical." However, some employer groups
have negotiated for such "gray areas" (health care items not reimbursed by Medicare), which increases the price for the consumer.
Traditional prosthetics are covered for 80 percent of the price.

Another for-profit HMO is also sponsored by a national insurance
organization. It has three centers in operation, none of which was
prepared to respond to this request. A representative from the public
relations department of the national headquarters did respond. Retired former employees can convert to individual policies and older
individuals can join. This company has an interesting system of payment for subscribers over age sixty-five. The enrollee with Medicare
turns all Medicare reimbursement over to the HMO and also pays
out of pocket the full individual premium, which is not reduced. Also,
the Medicare recipient is not eligible to use the HMO pharmacy,
which has a low flat charge for all prescribed medications. All Medicare recipients pay an add-on charge for each office visit and for all
emergency room visits. It appears that this company is "double dip-

ping," which the Commissioner of Insurance said is illegal, or that it is actively and aggressively discouraging those receiving Medicare from participating.

Two other HMOs will be discussed in more detail to indicate the different focus of for-profit and not-for-profit organizations. It should be remembered that the information on programs, services, and costs pertaining to both health maintenance organizations is limited to the years during which the information was collected. There have been changes since then. Health care programs and financing will continue to evolve over the next few years.

Health 1st Inc., an HMO functioning in this state, is a unit of the United HealthCare Corporation (UHC) based in Minnesota. The author was informed locally that the Health Care Financing Administration pays United to cover those over age sixty-five. However, these people need to pay a small monthly premium which covers much more than Medicare. The request for more information was relayed to the home office, which provided additional help.

A one-sheet overview of UHC in 1989 indicated it held a majority or wholly owned six HMOs for profit and also managed or partially owned twelve not-for-profit HMOs (United HealthCare Corporation 1989). Some plans covered examination for disabilities of interest here, but did not cover any appliances. A few covered hearing aids. Some Medicare plans required copayments for physician visits of five dollars per visit and emergency room copayments of twenty-five dollars. Most of these plans included prescribed medications, and some had other benefits as well. With regard to the disabilities of mobility and cognition, UHC followed the Medicare guidelines and provided therapies only if improvement of the patient could be documented. However, the promotional brochure of United's Share Senior Care for 1988 implied that Medicare provides "unlimited visits, paid in full" for home health care services, as does the UHC Share Senior Care plan (Schedule of Benefits #389 IL, 1988: 2–5). But Medicare caps the number of visits for home health care it will reimburse.

The 1987 UHC annual report (inside front cover) indicated "United HealthCare Corporation is a leader in the managed health care industry. Our primary business consists of owning and managing a national network of health maintenance organizations (HMOs)"— thirty-four in that year.

The operations review section of the annual report indicated UHC expected to shift focus from new HMO development to acquisitions and growth of their existing HMOs on the basis that the most successful companies "will be those with the product offerings, capabilities, and financial strength and flexibility to serve an ever more selective and demanding clientele." The clientele referred to were the customers of UHC, the employers.

Among the UHC HMOs, some were prepaid (capitated) but more were modified fee-for-service; some had open access and others had gatekeepers. In the capitation HMOs the physicians were paid a monthly fee; in the fee-for-service HMOs the physicians billed the HMO for their services and were paid according to a fee schedule. In order to strengthen this "business base," UHC planned to refocus to better meet the dictates of the marketplace. Some strategies for doing this in the HMOs owned by UHC "will include selective enrollment growth, reasonable pricing, and careful monitoring and adjustment of expense control."

In a special section on Medicare the report pointed out, "Our experience with capitation based Medicare products dates to 1979, when we participated in the government's early experiments with Medicare risk and cost sharing. Today Medicare is a profitable part of our business." They added, "The government increased by 13.5%, on average, its 1988 payments to HMOs providing health care coverage to Medicare members" (United HealthCare Corporation 1988: 5–7).

UHC also had a variety of other programs, or companies, relating to a variety of health care concerns. For example, the corporation was designing programs to help physicians lower their own expenses. UHC also had a pharmaceutical company which "markets our expertise in containing pharmaceutical costs." Other endeavors included specialty insurance companies, multiple-option health coverage and group life insurance, and a utilization review company which "services large self-insured employers, unions and insurance companies using many of the checks on quality and utilization employed in our HMOs." Cost-containment services were listed as well as the extensive data base and administration of third-party claims (United HealthCare Corporation 1988: 7–9).

The Kaiser Permanente plan has expanded across the country and now has ten centers in this state, where it is called the Kaiser Foundation Plan of Georgia, Inc. Kaiser is a capitation not-for-profit plan and has specific services for older people called Medicare Plus, which were current in 1989. Material on this plan is culled from promotional material for Medicare Plus in 1989.

Medicare Plus is available for individual subscription by a group member who converts after age sixty-five and to any other individual choosing this plan. The full monthly fee was reduced almost 75 percent to Medicare subscribers in 1989, subject to approval by the State Department of Insurance and the Health Care Financing Administration. The plan included basic HMO coverage in hospital and for outpatient care, plus outpatient allergy testing and treatment, vision and hearing examinations, short-term physical, speech, and occupational therapy, mental health up to forty-eight outpatient visits per year, up to thirty days of hospital care plus any additional days covered by Medicare, alcohol and drug detoxification care, durable medical equipment, and blood up to the Medicare coverage. It also evaluated cognitive and mobility problems. A dental plan was included with an office visit fee of twelve dollars and included examinations, prevention, and specialty consultations as needed. For all other necessary dental treatments the charges were 10 percent less than the usual and customary fees. The inclusion of preventive and early detection dental care at reduced fees and reduced fees for other dental procedures seems unique, in this state, for HMOs. Dental care for older persons is important in terms of self-image, communication, and nutrition. Too often, it is neglected by most forms of health insurance.

Home health care specified physician or nurse visits only when medically necessary. Up to 150 days in a skilled nursing facility was provided annually if medically necessary, including short-term physical, speech, and occupational therapy and inhalation therapy at no charge to the subscriber. The Kaiser Plan exclusions currently listed are hospice care and end-stage kidney disease. (brochure, Medicare Plus & Summary of Benefits, 1988).

A response from a former employee (1989) indicated Kaiser Permanente provided evaluations for mobility and cognitive problems directly or by referral to an appropriate specialist, as well as sight and hearing examinations. The HMO also provided treatment for "covered services" for these problems when coordinated, authorized, and arranged by the HMO physician. Hearing aids were not covered. The short-term physical and speech therapies were limited to treatment for conditions expected to show significant improvement within two months. The prostheses provided were those covered by Medicare. In the summary of benefits and services there is no mention of outpatient medicines or of other home-based therapies.

The annual report of United HealthCare Corporation, as an example of corporate-sponsored for-profit HMOs, documents claims made by Califano (1986: 212), Leyerle (1984: 111–113), and many articles in newspapers and popular magazines. It raises a number of questions about health care in general and HMOs in particular. An interesting point indicating the UHC focus in the 1987 annual report is the reference to health care as "a product" and cost containment of supplies for physicians as "a service." Can individual and groups of independent health professionals resist the pressures of resources and financial inducements offered by corporations? How much of the cost of Medicare to the federal government can be attributed to the profits of managed care corporations, to the profits of insurance companies sponsoring HMOs, to the profits of hospital chains? The answers to these questions would be a most interesting study.

Current regulations of peer review, utilization review, and diagnostic related groups (DRGs) dictate medical procedures to be used and length of hospital stay for each diagnosed patient, which are being made increasingly by business corporations in the health care field with governmental acquiescence (Leyerle 1984: 111). In light of this, is one of the original claims of HMOs of shortening hospital stays still valid? Is there a conflict of interest when "predominant financial support of hospitals, nursing homes [and HMOs which serve the over-sixty-five group] is governmental while the ownership remains predominantly private for profit" (Roemer 1982: 14)? Can the nonprofit capitated HMOs survive in the current corporate atmosphere in the face of both government and corporate pressure for cost containment as a prime goal?

The newest development is the social/health maintenance organization (S/HMO), discussed by Rivlin and Wiener (1988). This concept and demonstration was mandated by the Deficit Reduction Act of 1984. The Health Care Financing Administration has sponsored four S/HMOs: two by comprehensive chronic care agencies, one by a long-established nonprofit HMO, and one by a case management brokerage agency, each in a different section of the country.

S/HMOs broaden the concept of traditional HMOs to cover long-term care services not usually included, such as "a rich array of home care services." However, payment for institutionalization, when necessary, is limited to less than half the usual nursing home cost. The S/HMOs rely on case managers to control the utilization of chronic care benefits and guide patients to the less expensive level of benefit. A goal for each S/HMO is that membership reflect the distribution of disability among the local population at each site. This provides a mix of enrollees which helps to keep a financial balance in relation to the use of long-term services. Otherwise, exclusionary eligibility and selection requirements of S/HMOs may strongly reflect the need for profits in the privately sponsored S/HMOs. Rivlin and Wiener suggest:

> The future expansion of S/HMOs probably lies in two different strategies. First, they can function as "super medigap" policies that offer short and medium-term nursing home and home care. Second, they may develop as joint ventures between HMOs and insurance companies in which free standing long-term care insurance policies are sold to enrollees in HMOs. (Rivlin & Wiener 1988: 97–108 passim)

The interface of government support for profit and nonprofit health care services requires much vigorous research and study, far beyond the scope of this work. A broad question that applies to all kinds of private for-profit endeavors, including, but not limited to, health care, is implied in this work. To what degree should public funds raised by taxes be used to support organizations as profit-making endeavors?

CHAPTER 5

Implications

This work has looked at selected chronic health conditions of the elderly, focusing on their influence on both the micro and macro aspects of social living. This focus has been illuminated through examples wherever possible to dramatize the effects of these health problems on the person, the family, peers, activities of social living, involvement of concerned professionals beyond their job assignments, involvement of organizations or institutions, involvement of government at any level, and the involvement of health insurances.

The examples of beginning Alzheimer's and older adults with mental retardation indicate how important is it for both informal and formal care givers to be aware of cognitive problems in their early manifestations. The care givers also need to be understanding and/or knowledgeable about the expressed needs of the affected person in order to be most helpful in the early stages of Alzheimer's and long before the old age of the retarded person.

The examples of family care givers very clearly indicate the need for formal care givers to be aware of the needs of family members as well as knowledgeable about the health problems. Formal care givers need to be able to admit lack of knowledge and refer or consult appropriately, as needed.

Who the peers of the cognitively impaired are needs further exploration and study if social functioning while impaired is to be enhanced. Are the peers of Alzheimer patients those who were peers before the onset of this disease? Or are peers those who function at a similar social level at various stages of the disease? The same questions need to be raised about those with mental retardation. Are peers others of similar chronological age or those of similar functional ability? Adult day care centers are enhancing the social functioning and social outlets for cognitively impaired patients, which tends to carry over into the family social setting. The example of M. M. demonstrates that deinstitutionalization at age seventy-three after fifty years living within an institution can be successful if there is advanced planning by all professionals, with the person involved (surprises do not always produce positive results). Those primarily concerned with costs may question such use of staff time and energies. Is it still necessary to compare the cost of total public and private institutional care with a portion of professional time devoted to planning and preparation for communal living or enhanced home life? Are comparative studies in this area still needed?

Two examples of professional involvement in Alzheimer's disease and mental retardation beyond the usual parameters of job function are similar in the following ways. Each

1. Had specific goals for the social enhancement of clients' lives.

2. Planned out the steps necessary to achieve those goals.

3. Involved other professional disciplines and/or organizations administratively and programmatically in the planning and acceptance of the goals.

4. Showed flexibility while developing the program.

5. Encouraged upgrading and recognition of the value and services of workers in these programs.

6. Initiated groundwork for continuation of these needed programs.

These six steps in initiating interagency collaboration and in developing a needed service might function as one model to develop, enhance, or enlarge services to an underserved population.

For organizations involved with cognitive disability, a small local example and a successful national one were selected, although the influence of each was different. The similarities in both involved their processes and interdisciplinary and educational foci.

Questions need to be raised about each. Did the effects of the smaller project on the community continue after the demonstration ended? Did it stimulate other organizations serving a different population to apply for similar demonstration grants? Did the involved public department use its success to continue the particular demonstration or to develop others? When comprehensive attention is paid to all the needs of a select population, the gaps in comprehensive long-term care are exposed. These questions lead to questions about the current amount, quality, and adequacy of care available, accessible, and affordable.

On the other hand, the national organization started with the advantage of having experienced business people, who involved knowledgeable specialists and hired a public relations firm to influence policymakers in Congress. The efforts of this group has influenced the macro parts of society through much wider knowledge and understanding of Alzheimer's disease and much more funding for research. Perhaps most importantly, it has influenced Congress to consider and recognize this disease and some insurance companies to consider coverage. National health organizations tend to follow the medical model of specialization and focus on one chronic health problem to expand areas of research and care. However, this leads to competition among all national health organizations for public attention, funds, and volunteers. How can such competition be minimized in the economic and political structure of free-enterprise capitalism? Are there alternative ways of allotting resources not yet explored? For example, is it possible for the proportion of resources for each chronic disease to be based on the number of people with each condition?

A local chapter of a service organization was able to educate and influence a state legislative subcommittee in its deliberations over long-term care insurance. The involvement of knowledgeable experts and consumers, careful amassing of background information, collection of current data within the state, and thoughtful deliberation by the study committee and its reasonable conclusions all contributed to its influence on the legislature. Hopefully, this example can stimulate thinking and planning in other communities to deal with the need for long-term care insurance.

Older people with hearing loss often are not properly diagnosed until the problem is far advanced. Can this be due to cursory physical examination by physicians, who may not have been trained to notice beginning symptoms, or when educated as specialists, tend not to hear patients' other complaints? Patients, after all, have lived with their own bodies for many years and often notice changes in their functioning, which still may be very close to age-specific norms. Does this suggest that a changed focus is needed in physicians' education, especially as the number of older patients increases? Lack of early diagnosis may be due also to denial, fear, projection, or to other emotional and social reasons by persons with hearing loss.

Examples used in this work involve men who were very aware of their condition but had to go through a long period and a number of physicians to find the most effective help. Early accurate diagnoses are particularly advantageous now that there are a variety of methods available to correct or minimize the condition.

Remedial help for loss of hearing ought to be geared to family members also, because their understanding and attitudes are crucial to the reactions, attitudes, and functioning of the deafened one. The two examples indicate the difference in family acceptance of hearing loss. Notwithstanding the differing personalities and life histories of the two men, the approaches and attitudes of their respective spouses influenced their perception of themselves as functioning individuals. The principles outlined by P. Ashley (1985: 71–75) can be utilized by professional disciplines as well as by families when dealing with persons of any age with hearing loss.

Peer relationships obviously change with hearing loss. It was inevitable that Mr. D.'s associates and some friends would fall away with his withdrawal from social life. Until his attendance at the Audio Education Center, he made no effort to develop new contacts. Mr. K., on the other hand, was able to change his employment after his hearing loss, made some new social contacts, went to church dances—where he met his current wife—and still participates in group activities. These two men very clearly indicate the need for formal care givers to learn as much as possible about the interests, life history, and comprehensive needs of patients before the disability disrupts their lives, to encourage them to live as fully as possible with the disability.

The social functioning of people with late onset hearing loss can vary widely, although it may be more curtailed than their previous social functioning. Enlarging and enhancing opportunities for social functioning may be a fruitful area for education research. Recent technological advances in communication devices, such as TDD telephones and the audio loop, are tremendous aids in this area. Other developments like sight signals in addition to bells and buzzers also enhance the safety and ego building aspects of living with hearing loss. Hopefully, the costs of all such aids will be reduced, making them available to all who need them.

The statewide self-help council is one example of a growing trend among people with disabilities to be known and accepted as complete, independent, fully functioning adults. The council was the only example found relating to hearing loss in which professional involvement extended beyond the parameters of the job functions. The process of forming the council and involving many groups throughout the state to influence legislators clearly highlights the strong motivation and determination to succeed necessary to bring such a complex undertaking to fruition.

The organizational example, SHHH, most probably owes its successful development to the driving force and determination of its founder, Howard Stone. In his account of its development he used every avenue open to him to help publicize his concerns and propagate his ideas. SHHH has grown tremendously in a short time. However, it appears that the full interdisciplinary interaction and collaboration necessary to effect macro change somehow did not meld very effectively. Is this because of the singularly strong personality of its founder; or because of the variety of already developed national organizations which focus on part of the total problem and prefer not to share or give up their "turf"; or is it due to the generally held belief that lack of hearing is not as catastrophic as some other chronic problems? Comprehensive studies as to why and how some national health organizations become "popular" and seem to attract public and private research resources would be an interesting area for research.

The first example of lack of mobility indicates a myriad of problems in the home, not all of which can be addressed by any home health agency, even with case managers. Case management, case coordination, or managed health care are the latest terms for work that some social workers, some public health nurses, and some discharge planners in hospitals have been performing for years as an integral part of their jobs. Only now, as some social workers have said, "We give it a title and get paid for these functions that we used to give away for free." Nonprofit social agencies are using this method to generate more income. Private for-profit health care chains, especially those involved in managed care plans, are using case management to cut costs by preventing overutilization of resources. Private for-profit case management businesses are mushrooming. All this is part of the privatization of health and social service care, especially focused on elderly people.

Case management, as such, is "the coordination of a specified group of resources and services for a specified group of people" (Kane 1988: 5). Basically, it consists of case finding or screening, comprehensive, multidimensional assessment, care planning, implementation of the plan, monitoring, and formal reassessment (Kane 1988: 6). The case manager is expected to be both an advocate for the client and gatekeeper of resources. Additionally and increasingly, in this period of scarce resources and spiraling costs, case managers are expected to arrange for services with cost containment as an important focus. This pertains in public as well as in private health care and other private organizations. A full, multidimensional exploration, including costs and ethical considerations, of case management can be found in the fall 1988 issue of *Generations*. Quality case management implies, at the least, an awareness of the need for resources from a variety of disciplines other than the case manager's (Kane 1988: 77–78). In one example used in this work, the need for a dental evaluation was obvious, as were some form of respite for the daughter-in-law and transportation for medical needs.

The rehabilitation team in the second example did stress the need, after discharge, for the type of therapy the rehabilitation center provided. However, no one in the family meeting mentioned the possibility of other communal supports for the patient and the daughter with whom the patient would live.

Hopefully, these lacks will be remedied by the increasing focus on interdisciplinary study and training in gerontology, especially in higher education. The theme of the fifteenth annual meeting of the Association for Gerontology in Higher Education in March 1989 was interdisciplinary learning both in classrooms and practicums. Papers from eight sessions that seemed most appropriate to this work were requested, and most authors responded.

It was most interesting to read the paper by Dr. Arthur Van Stewart and the article in *Aging Network News* by Van Stewart and Furnish (1989: 15–16, 20) and find that schools of dentistry, for the most part, have not been included in interdisciplinary teams of educators in the area of gerontology. The historical lack of attention to the dental needs of older people also was reflected by the staff of the home health agency in the example of mobility. Yet good oral health is very important for older people for adequate nutritional needs, for better communication with others, and for self-esteem and ego strength. Hopefully, the clarion call in Dr. Stewart's paper and article has alerted other professional disciplines to the importance of good oral health for older people.

Another paper of particular interest, presented by Dr. David Satin, raises many basic issues when academia attempts to integrate and sustain an interdisciplinary department in a university setting, especially in the study of gerontology. In addition to providing a unique sample of interdisciplinary education in aging, Satin also specifies the "attitudinal and organizational barriers" to it and to gerontology found in academic institutions and their administrations. Satin addresses, in academia, factors that Cotten and Wentworth (1987: 4–6) stressed about attitudes and lack of knowledge of staff and administrators when integrating older retarded persons into mainstream aging activities. Rose and Ansello (1987: 25–27) found the same prejudices and lack of knowledge in their research study in Maryland at all levels of public, governmental, and private agency staff and administrations. Both Cotten and Rose and Ansello found "cross-fertilization" of attitudes and knowledge between the fields of the developmentally disabled aged and aging was imperative before integration of policy could be initiated and sustained on an institutional scale. Based on Satin's paper the same type of comments can be made about academic disciplines unwilling to reduce their "turf" or accept on a co-equal basis input from other disciplines, or accept the need for both compromise and collaboration to organize and sustain an interdisciplinary department of gerontology effectively.

This work presents a first step by which unidisciplinary respect for interdisciplinary input can increase comprehension and appreciation of both academicians and practitioners when the patient/client is viewed holistically in personal, social, and communal life.

SOME PRACTICES NEEDING CHANGE

If the goal of optimal social functioning of the chronically disabled is acceptable, a number of past and current attitudes and practices of education, health care, and social service providers need to be examined, rearranged, changed, and/or discarded.

All health care and social service providers need to understand it is the patients/clients who are most familiar with the reactions and normal functioning of their own bodies. Formal service providers need to listen to and hear the complaints, explanations, and questions of the patient and the family. Often the latter may be able to add helpful information. Health and social histories limited to written material or computer screening only cannot provide the insight to help a particular person. Even though it is more time consuming and labor intensive for face-to-face collection of material, it is imperative in order to comprehend the wholeness of the person. Professional social service workers, public health nurses, therapists, and aides usually use dialogue with the patient more than institutional staff. This is one practice that needs to be encouraged and developed among staffs, including physicians, outpatient clinics, acute care hospitals, nursing homes, rehabilitation centers, and other long-term care institutions.

After the history is documented, listening to the patient/client and family is particularly important with chronic health problems, which vary in development and intensity over time and in changed circumstances. Allowing the time to listen implies a change in attitudes and historical roles, especially by administrators and physicians. The historical role of physician autonomy has changed over the last two decades (Leyerle 1984: 23–24, 36–39; Califano 1986: 186, 200–201), but not in favor of the patient. The physician now is limited by the necessity to conform to PRO, DRG regulations and other cost-cutting control devices, including the amount of time spent with each patient. Physical, occupational, and speech therapists and home visiting nurses are limited to services to enable the patient to "reach optimal functioning" or until the patient is "stabilized" and the family has "learned how to" maintain him/her. Reimbursement for social workers in home health agencies is limited to two home visits per patient. These professional staff members are limited by the reimbursement provided by both public and private insurers. Moreover, their services are available only when ordered by a physician, who may not be aware of the patient's total living situation.

Another area needing change is work time permitted by administrators and funding bodies to the formal care givers for linkage activity between the patient and the needed service. For example, it takes time, and frequently numerous telephone calls, to make an effective referral, and then more time for the necessary follow-up. This is not considered cost effective by the budgetary gurus, and therefore no money is allotted for the time for this necessary service. Follow-up on referrals often can be done by paraprofessionals or volunteers. The best services in the world do no one any good if they are not accessible, available, and affordable to those who need them.

Another area requiring change is the attitudes of some formal care givers toward the person who has a disability. Pity, hopeless resignation, or repugnance is not helpful to the disabled. A patient in a hospital is not necessarily a helpless, completely dependent blob to be poked, pulled, pushed, pricked, and/or physically invaded by a myriad of professional strangers. Explanations of procedures often are helpful to the patient and family members. This can result in better compliance. Additionally, many professionals (and politicians) use the patient's first name in an effort to be friendly. Friendship is a mutual relationship, between people on an equal footing. How would the health care professionals react if patients used their first names in an effort to be friendly in return? When the first name is used only by the formal care giver it appears to be patronizing, condescending, or pitying. These generalizations about the use of first names are most applicable when the people do not know one another. They also do not take into account regional, ethnic, or religious mores.

Many patients/clients, particularly with a chronic disability, live with family members or have family members who are very involved with helping them to function. Some family care givers may be biased in their feelings about the expectations for the chronically disabled, but they tend to know the habits and functioning of the disabled person more intimately than formal care givers. Additionally, they will continue to be intimately involved with that person after hospitalization or therapy is completed. Therefore, decisions about and particularly results of treatments, therapies, and procedures are important for them. Care givers need to know the results of medical and psychosocial interventions in order to help the person carry out necessary routines and function at maximum capacity. If family care givers are excluded either inadvertently or deliberately, if their questions are not considered seriously, they may, also either inadvertently or deliberately, thwart or undo the progress that was made by the formal care givers.

In all the material cited previously, and in all public utterances and readings, one area of health care—costs—has been almost universally omitted. At the risk of stating a quixotic theory without any research, please seriously consider the practicality of putting a cap on the percentage of profits allowable to pharmaceutical companies, private enterprises that provide supplies to facilities and physicians, private hospital chains, manufacturers of hi-tech equipment used by physicians and facilities, private managed care businesses, and health insurance companies.

All of these entities add immeasurably to the cost of health care because of their need for profits, their individual administrative costs, their individual advertising costs, and the perks many of them provide to the formal care givers. There are caps put on interest rates for loans and interest rates to bank depositors. Insurance companies are required to maintain a certain level of assets in many states. Stipulations and limits are required of many forms of business—why not a limit on the percentage of profits in health care? Obviously, this is a very complex issue which has not been addressed, as yet, by policymakers, governmental bodies, and profit-making concerns. But is it ethical to profit from the sickness of other people? Attention to this has been found in only one article (Holstein 1989: 61–64), which raises six fundamental questions.

1. Is it ethical to make a profit from ill health?
2. Does social responsibility to distribute health care to all conflict with free-market distribution?
3. Is health care designed to serve profits, providers, or people? Can these ends be compatible? Can they be balanced?
4. How do inadequate public benefits help create new needs and (in the case of aging) how do these inadequacies prey on elders' fears?

5. Why, when we speak of cost containment, is the focus not on profits and an expensive, fragmented system but on those dependent on the system, including elders?

6. Why are market principles so difficult to apply to health care, and why, when applied, do they often cause perverse results?

These are the kinds of questions ethicists, universities, think tanks, politicians, governmental bodies, educators, and practitioners of health care and social services should be discussing toward the goals of resolving the problems mentioned above in favor of the patient/consumer. A resource in this area of health care is the Public Citizen Health Research Group–sponsored *Health Letter,* edited by Dr. Sidney M. Wolfe, which publishes questionable business practices of physicians, drug companies and health care facilities. To my knowledge, this group has not been sued for libel.

This is a time of discussion about "cost cutting," "cost containment," "basic health care vs. full-spectrum healthcare," "public vs. private sponsorship," "competition for health care," "blaming the victim," "profit vs. social good," and "health care as a right." Ethical norms for care by all involved players must include compassion, cooperation, and collaboration to achieve the highest level of health and social integration possible. This implies changes in attitudes, methods, and goals from competition, and high profits to cooperation, innovation, and collaboration by all facets of society to achieve constructive social goals. Is there enough pressure from the uninsured and the chronically disabled and their families to move such a mountain? Can it be achieved incrementally? If this work helps to stimulate discussion and/or action by the chronically disabled and their families and by the many disciplines involved in their care and lives, it will have served a useful purpose.

Bibliography

Adams, P., & Benson, V. (December 1992). Current estimates from the national health interview survey, 1991. In *Vital and Health Statistics,* Series 10, No. 184. DHHS Public Health Service, Centers for Disease Control, National Center for Health Statistics, Government Printing Office.

Administration on Aging. (January 1988). Compendium of aging active grants under title IV of the older Americans act, active in FY 1987 (October). Shared by the Regional Office, Administration on Aging, Atlanta.

Alpert, M. (Spring 1983). What care do the caregivers need? Paper presented at the Southern Gerontological Society annual meeting, Atlanta.

Arthritis Foundation. (1984). *A serious look at the facts* (pamphlet). Atlanta: Public Education Department, the Arthritis Foundation.

Ashley, J. (1985). A personal account. In H. Orlans (Ed.), *Adjustment to adult hearing loss.* Research Institute & U. S. Commission on Civil Rights. San Diego: College Hill Press.

Ashley, P. (1985). Deafness in the family. In H. Orlans (Ed.), *Adjustment to adult hearing loss.* Gallaudet Research Institute & U. S. Commission on Civil Rights. San Diego: College Hill Press.

Association for Gerontology in Higher Education 15th annual meeting (March 2–5, 1989). Abstracts. Tampa, FL.

Bankoff, E. A. (1983). Aged parents and their widowed daughters: A support relationship. *Journal of Gerontology* 38 (2).

Beck, John C., Benson, D. F., Scheibel, A. B., Spar, J. E., & Rubenstein, L. Z. (1982). Dementia in the elderly: The silent epidemic. *Annals of Internal Medicine* 99 (2).

Becker, G. (1980). *Growing old in silence*. Berkeley and Los Angeles: University of California Press.

Berkow, R. (Ed.). (1982). *The Merck manual of diagnosis and therapy*. 14th ed. Vol. 1. Rahway, NJ: Merck, Sharp & Dohme Research Laboratories.

Besdine, R. W. (1982). Dementia. In J. W. Rowe & R. W. Besdine (Eds.), *Health and disease in old age*. Boston: Little Brown.

Beyond Medicare, what insurance do you need? (June 1989). *Consumer Reports* 55 (6).

Black, W. F., & Paddison, R. M. (1984). Neurobehavioral changes in the aged. In H. Rothschild (Ed.), C. F. Chapman (Coordinating Ed.). *Risk factors for senility*. New York: Oxford University Press.

Bonner, C. (1974). *Homburger and Bonner's medical care and rehabilitation of the aged and chronically ill* (3rd ed.). Boston: Little Brown.

Brindle, J. (January 1969). Prospects for prepaid group practice. *American Journal of Public Health* 59. Supplement, Medical Care: The current scene and prospects for the future, Part II. Proceedings of symposium in honor of I. S. Falk, Ph.D FAPHA. Yale University School of Medicine for the American Public Health Association.

Brown, J.H.D. (1978). *The politics of health care*. Cambridge, MA: Ballinger.

Burns, E. M. (1971). Health care systems. In R. Morris (Ed.-in-Chief), *Encyclopedia of Social Work 1* (16).

Califano, J. A. (1986). *American health care revolution. Who lives? Who dies? Who pays?* New York: Random House.

Castillo, H. M., & Hall, D. C. (September 1987). Discharge planning needs for hip fractures: A descriptive study. *Journal of Applied Gerontology* 6 (3).

Center for Rehabilitation Medicine. (1987). *In celebration of the tenth anniversary of the opening of the Center for Rehabilitation Medicine, 1977–1987* (brochure). Atlanta: Emory University Hospital.

Cohen, P. (May–June 1983). A group approach for working with families of the elderly. *The Gerontologist 23* (3).

Challenge grant received for establishment of ADRDA respite care program (Winter 1984). *ADRDA Newsletter* 4 (4). Chicago, IL.

Cotten, P. D., & Wentworth, R. (October 16, 1987). Final narrative report of the Mississippi elderly developmentally disabled persons project. Funded by the Developmented Disabilities Funds provided through the Bureau of Mental Retardation, Mississippi Department of Mental Health; presented to the Bureau of Mental Retardation, Mississippi Department of Mental Health.

Coye, J. A. (January 1988). There's nothing like hands-on. *Atlanta Area Chapter ADRDA Newsletter.*

Estes, C. L., & Lee, P. R. (1985). Social, political and economic background of long-term care policy. In C. Harrington, R. J. Newcomer, C. L. Estes & Associates (Eds.), *Long-term care of the elderly: Public policy issues.* Beverly Hills, CA: Sage Publications.

Federal Register (December 30, 1987). Part II, Department of Health and Human Services: Office of Human Development Services: FY 1988. Coordinated Discretionary Funds Program (52) 250. Washington, DC: U.S. Government Printing Office.

Garstecki, D. C. (1987). A multidisciplinary approach: The role of ancillary personnel. In J. Alpiner & P. McCarthy (Eds.), *Rehabilitative audiology.* Baltimore: Williams & Wilkins.

The Georgia consortium on the psychology of aging (n.d.). Brochure distributed at the 1990 annual meeting of the Georgia Gerontology Society.

Ginzberg, E. (1985). *American medicine: The power shift.* Totowa, NJ: Roman & Allanheld.

————. (1988). United States health policy: Expectations and realities. *Journal of the American Medical Association* 260 (24).

Glass, L. E. (1985). Psychosocial aspects of hearing loss in adulthood. In H. Orlans (Ed.), *Adjustment to adult hearing loss.* Gallaudet Research Institute & U.S. Commission on Civil Rights. San Diego: College Hill Press.

Glassman, M. (1980). Misdiagnosis of senile dementia: denial of care to the elderly. *Social Work, Journal of the National Association of Social Workers* 25 (4).

Goldman, A. (1989). Long term care insurance regulations update. *Georgia Gerontology Society Newsletter* 15 (1).

Greenberg, H. (1982). And Sara laughed. In *Rites of passage.* New York: Avon Books.

Griffith, D. (June 1986). Blending key ingredients to assure quality in home health care. *Nursing and Health Care* 7 (6).

Gross-Andrew, S., & Zimmer, A. H. (1978). Incentives to families caring for disabled elderly: Research and demonstration project to strengthen the natural support system. *Journal of Gerontological Social Work* 1 (2).

Haber, D. (May–June 1983). Promoting mutual help groups among older persons. *The Gerontologist* 23 (3).

Harrington, C., Estes, C. L., Lee, P. R., & Newcomer, R. J. (1985). State policies in long term care. In C. Harrington, R. J. Newcomer, C. L. Estes & Associates (Eds.), *Long-term care of the elderly: Public policy issues.* Beverly Hills, CA: Sage Publications.

Health Care Financing Administration (n.d.). *Catastrophic protection and other new benefits: An official notice to Medicare beneficiaries explaining benefits under the Medicare catastrophic act of 1988.* Department of Health and Human Services, Health Care Financing Administration. Baltimore: Official Business.

Holstein, M. (1989). Business and aging, what's the concern? *Generations* 13 (3).

Illsley, R. (1981). Problems of dependency groups: The care of the elderly, the handicapped and the chronically ill. Part II. *Social Science and Medicine* 15A (3). Pergamon Press Ltd.

The in-home respite program (September 1985). *Atlanta Area Chapter, ADRDA Newsletter.*

Initial assessment tool (October 1987). Atlanta Area Chapter ADRDA, paper presented at the Georgia Gerontology Society annual meeting.

Janicki, M. P. (August 1986). Growing old: Responding to the needs of older and elderly persons with developmental disabilities: Suggestions for state and area agencies activities in the area of aging and developmental disabilities. Report to the national training conference of the National Association of State Units on Aging and National Association of Area Agencies on Aging, Seattle, WA.

Jennings, J. (1987). Elderly parents as caregivers for their adult dependent children. *Social Work, Journal of the National Association of Social Workers* 32 (5).

Johnston, M. (1984). Psychological aspects of chronic disease. In J. Hasler & T. Schofield (Eds.), *Continuing care: The management of chronic disease.* Oxford General Practice Series, 7. London: Oxford University Press.

Kahn, C. R., & J. F. R. [*sic*] (1985). The scientific network. *Joslin Magazine* 1 (3). Boston: Joslin Diabetes Center.

Kaiser Foundation Health Plan of Georgia, Inc. (1988). *Medicare plus: Summary of benefits 1988* (brochure). Atlanta: Kaiser Foundation.

Kaiser Permanente. (1988). *Introducing you to Kaiser Permanente Medicare plus* (pamphlet). Kaiser Foundation Health Plan, Inc.

Kane, R. (Guest Ed.) (Fall 1988). Introduction; Case management: what next? *Generations XII* (5).

Kaplan, H. (1985). Benefits and limitations of amplification and speechreading for the elderly. In H. Orlans (Ed.), *Adjustment to adult hearing loss.* Gallaudet Research Institute & U.S. Commission on Civil Rights. San Diego: College Hill Press.

Kerson, T. S., with Kerson, L. (1985). *Understanding chronic illness: The medical and psychosocial dimensions of nine diseases.* New York and London: The Free Press.

Krauss, M. W., & Selzer, M. M. (1986). National survey of programs serving elderly mentally retarded persons: A summary report of findings. Project conducted by Brandeis University, The Starr Center for Mental Retardation, The Eunice Kennedy Shriver Center, and Boston University School of Social Work.

Lederer, L. (March–April 1991). Finding common ground. *The OWL Observer,* national newspaper of the Older Women's League.

Lee, D. V. (July 10, 1985). Memorandum to members of the Georgia Senate long term care insurance study committee. [Used with written permission from Lee.]

Leyerle, B. (1984). *Moving and shaking American medicine: The structure of a socioeconomic transformation.* Westport, CT: Greenwood Press.

Louey, H. S., & Per-Lee, M. S. (1983). *What do I do now? Problems and adaptations of the deafened adult.* Washington, DC: National Academy of Gallaudet College.

Lyons, W. (1982). Coping with cognitive impairment: Some family dynamics and helping roles. *Journal of Gerontological Social Work* 4 (3–4).

Mace, N. L., & Rabins, P. V. (1981). *The 36-hour day.* Baltimore: Johns Hopkins University Press.

Marples, M. (1986). Helping family members cope with a senile relative. *Social Casework, Journal of Contemporary Social Work* 67 (8).

McCarthy, P. A. (1987). Rehabilitation of the hearing impaired geriatric client. In J. Alpiner & P. A. McCarthy (Eds.), *Rehabilitative audiology: Children and adults.* Baltimore: Williams & Wilkins.

McGinnis, F., & Midura, H. (December 1985). Alzheimer's disease study committee report. Georgia Department of Human Resources Office of Aging. Atlanta: Georgia Department of Human Resources.

McKenzie, L. H. (December 1985). Report of the Georgia Senate private long-term care insurance study committee. Distributed to the Governor, Lieutenant Governor, Speaker of the House of Representatives, members of the General Assembly of Georgia, and other interested persons.

Meadow-Orlans, K. P. (1985). Social and psychological effects of hearing loss in adulthood: A literature review. In H. Orlans (Ed.), *Adjustment to adult hearing loss.* Gallaudet Research Institute & U.S. Commission on Civil Rights. San Diego: College Hill Press.

Medicaid guide (n.d.). Distributed by the Georgia Department of Medical Assistance, Atlanta.

The Medicare handbook (1990). U.S. Department of Health & Human Services, Health Care Financing Administration, Pub. No. HCFA 10050.

Myers, B. A. (April 1971). Health maintenance organizations: Objectives and issues. Speech delivered at annual conference of state comprehensive health planning agencies, Washington, DC.

Naisbitt, J. (1982). *Megatrends.* New York: Warner Books.

National Center for Health Statistics (December 1991). Current estimates from the National Health Interview Survey, 1990. Series 10, No. 181 USDHHS, Public Health Service, Center for Disease Control. Hyattsville, MD: US Government Printing Office.

National Institute on Aging (1983). *Age page: Hearing and the elderly.* U.S. Department of Health and Human Service, Public Health Service, NIH, U.S. Government Printing Office.

―――. (1983). *National Institute on Aging.* DHHS, NIA NIH Publication No. 83-1129. Revised July 1983. Bethesda, MD.

―――. (1987). *Research advances in aging 1984–1986.* DHHS, Public Health Service, NIA NIH Publication No. 87-2862. Bethesda, MD.

―――. (May 1988). Statement on the purposes and main foci of the NIA. Bethesda, MD: National Institute of Health.

―――. (1988). ADRES Report ACT 100 BSR active and obligated grants and contracts by principal investigator (12/1/87). Shared by the NIA Office of Information, Bethesda, MD.

Neugarten, B. L. (1983). Aging: Social policy issues for the developed countries. In M. Bergener, J. Lehn, E. Land, & R. Schmitz-Scherzer (Eds.), *Aging in the eighties and beyond.* New York: Springer.

Newcomer, R. J., Benjamin, H. E., Jr., & Sattler, C. E. (1985). Equity and incentives in medical program eligibility. In C. Harrington, R. J. Newcomer, C. L. Estes & Associates (Eds.), *Long-term care of the elderly: Public policy issues.* Beverly Hills, CA: Sage Publications.

Olson, L., Caton, C., & Duffy, M. (1981). *The elderly and the future economy.* Lexington, MA: Lexington Books.

Palley, H. A., & Oktay, J. S. (1983). *The chronically limited elderly: The case for a national policy for in-home and supportive community-based services.* New York: Haworth Press.

Pechansky, R., Safford, B. M., & Simmons, H. (1968). Medical practice in a group setting: The Russellton experience. In R. Pechansky (Ed.), *Health services administration: Policy cases and the case method.* Cambridge: Harvard University Press.

Pedigo, N. W., Jr. (1984). Drug therapy as a risk factor for senility. In H. Rothchild (Ed.), *Risk factors for senility.* New York: Oxford University Press.

Poe, W. D. (1969). *The old person in your home.* New York: Charles Scribner's Sons.

Proposal, Community Service Center for the Hearing Impaired (March 24, 1988). Prepared by the Georgia Council for the Hearing Impaired. Shared with the full consent of the Executive Board.

Respite registry to begin (April 1987). *Atlanta Area Chapter ADRDA Newsletter.*

Rich, B. M., & Baum, M. (1984). *The aging: A guide to public policy.* Pittsburgh: University of Pittsburgh Press.

Rinke, L. T. (June 1987). A vital new paradigm. *Nursing and Health* 8 (6).

Rivlin, A. M., & Wiener, J. M., with Hanley, R. J., & Spence, D. A. (1988). *Caring for the disabled elderly. Who will pay?* Washington, DC: Brookings Institution.

Roemer, M. I. (1982). *An introduction to the United States health care system.* New York: Springer Publishing Co.

Roosevelt Warm Springs Institute for Rehabilitation (n.d.). *General information for referral and admission.* Warm Springs, GA: Department of Human Resources, Division of Rehabilitation Services.

Roosevelt Warm Springs Institute for Rehabilitation (n.d.). *The medical rehabilitation unit.* Warm Springs, GA: Department of Human Resources, Division of Rehabilitation Services.

Rose, T. (1988). *Aging and developmental disabilities from A–Z.* Available from Dr. Thomas Rose, Center on Aging, University of Maryland.

Rose, T., & Ansello, E. (1987). *Aging and developmental disabilities: Research and planning.* Final report to the Maryland State Planning Council on Developmental Disabilities. The National Center on Aging and Disabilities, Center on Aging. College Park, MD: The University of Maryland.

Rose, T., & Janicki, M. P. (1986). Older developmentally disabled adults: A forgotten population. *Aging Network News* 111 (5).

Rosen, G. (1958). *A history of public health.* New York: MD Publications.

Rosser, J. M., & Mossberg, H. E. (1977). *An analysis of health care delivery.* New York: John Wiley & Sons.

Rowland, D. (1990). Fewer resources, greater burdens: Medical care coverage for low income elderly people. In J. D. Rockefeller IV (chairman). The Pepper Commission on Comprehensive Health Care, Supplement to the final report September 1990. Washington, DC: U.S. Government Printing Office.

Ruscio, D., & Cavarocchi, N. (1984). Getting on the political agenda. *Generations* 9 (2).

Safford, B. (1968). Changing a community pattern of medical care. In R. Pechansky (ed.). *Health services administration: Policy cases and the case method.* Cambridge: Harvard University Press.

Satin, D. (1989). Overcoming academic attitudinal and organizational barriers to interdisciplinary education in aging. Paper presented at 15th annual meeting, Association for Gerontology in Higher Education, Tampa, FL (March 5, 1989).

Sela, I. (1986). A study of programs and services for the hearing impaired elderly in senior centers and clubs in the U.S.A. Gallaudet Research Institute. Study funded in part by the National Institute of Handicapped Research, U.S. Department of Education.

Shaw, S. B. (1987). Parental aging: Clinical issues in adult psychotherapy. *Social Casework* 68 (7).

Sidel, V. W., & Sidel, R. (1977). *A healthy state: An international perspective on the crisis in United States medical care.* New York: Pantheon Books.

Silverstone, B., & Hyman, H. K. (1976). *You and your aging parent.* New York: Pantheon Books.

Simon, J. (1979). Multicategorical approach to chronic disease. In *Public policy and chronic disease.* National Arthritis Advisory Board Forum, NIA Pub. #79-1986. U.S. Department of HEW, Public Health Service.

Southern Bell. (no date provided). *Telecommunication services for people with special needs.* Bellsouth Co.

Stafford, F. (1980). A program for families of the mentally impaired elderly, *The Gerontologist 20* (6).

Stern, C. (August 2, 1987). Do you lose your balance? *Parade.* New York: Parade Publications, Inc.

Stoesz, D. (July–August 1986). Corporate welfare: The third state of welfare in the United States. *Social Work, The Journal of NASW* 31 (4).

Stoller, E. P., & Earl, L. L. (1983). Help with activities of daily life: Sources of support for the non-institutionalized elderly. *The Gerontologist* 23 (1).

Stone, H. (1985). Developing SHHH, a self-help organization. In H. Orlans (ed.). *Adjustment to adult hearing loss.* Gallaudet Research Institute & U.S. Commission on Civil Rights. San Diego: College Hill Press.

Stone, J. H. (1982). The self-help movement: Organizing a national organization. *Generations* 7 (1).

They grow old too (n.d.). Brochure the Mississippi Elderly Developmentally Disabled Project.

Trager, B. (1986). Home care and public policy. *Caring, ABCs of Home Care* 5 (8).

United HealthCare Corporation. (1988). *Annual report: 1987.* Minneapolis: United HealthCare.

———. (1988). *Schedule of benefits for groups: Share senior care* (brochure). Minneapolis: United HealthCare.

———. (1989). Overview of United HealthCare Corporation (printed fact sheet). Minneapolis: United HealthCare.

United States Department of Health Education and Welfare (December

1973). *HMO questions physicians are asking about HMOs and the answers.* DHEW PHS Health Services and Mental Health Administration, Health Maintenance Organization Service. DHEW Publication No. (HSM) 73-13009. Washington, DC: U.S. Government Printing Office.

Van Stewart, A., & Furnish, G. M. (1989). Dentistry: Becoming more committed to the delivery of oral health services for the aged. *Aging Network News* 5 (12).

Van Stewart, A., Thibault, J. M., & Stewart, J. F. (1989). Schools of Dentistry: An increasingly important resource for geriatric education programs. Paper presented at the 15th annual meeting, Association for Gerontology in Higher Education, Tampa, FL, (March 4, 1989).

Van Tuyl, L. (August 1987). Preventing isolation and cognitive decline. *Atlanta Area Chapter ADRDA Newsletter.*

Warner, H. C. (1987). Community service centers for deaf people: Where are we now? *American Annals of the Deaf* 132 (3).

Wax, T., & DiPietro, L. (1987). *Managing hearing loss in later life.* Gallaudet University. Washington, DC: National Information Center on Deafness/American Speech-Language-Hearing Association.

Weeks, J. R., & Cuellar, J. B. (1981). The role of family members in the helping networks of older people. *The Gerontologist* 21 (4).

Weiler, P. G. (1987). The public health impact of Alzheimer's disease. *American Journal of Public Health* 77 (9).

Who can afford a nursing home? (May 1988). *Consumer Reports* 54 (5).

Williams, P. S. (1987). *Hearing loss: Information for professionals in the aging network.* Rockville, MD: American Speech-Language-Hearing Association.

Wolfe, S. M., (Ed.). *Health Letter,* Public Citizen Health Research Group, 2000 P. Street, Washington, DC.

World Health Organization. (1985). *Mental retardation: Meeting the challenge.* (Offset Publication No. 86. Prepared in collaboration with the Joint Commission on International Aspects of Mental Retardation.) Geneva: World Health Organization.

Zarit, S. H., Reever, K. E., & Back-Peterson, J. (1980). Relatives of the impaired elderly: Correlates of feelings of burdens. *The Gerontologist* 20 (6).

Zawadski, R. T. (1984). The long term care demonstration projects: What they are and why they came into being. In R. T. Zawadski (Ed.), *Community-based systems of long term care.* New York: Haworth Press.

Zigler, E. (June 1988). The IQ pendulum. (Review of *The raising of intelli-*

gence: A selected history of attempts to raise retarded intelligence, by Herman H. Spitz.) *Readings: A Journal of Reviews and Commentary in Mental Health* 3 (2). New York: American Orthopsychiatric Association.

Index

Activities of daily living (ADL), 88, 90, 92

Activities of social functioning: definition, 23; and hearing loss, 64–65; and mental retardation, 24–26; and motor disability, 94–95

Adams, Patricia and Veronica Benson (National Health Interview Survey in Division of Health Interview Statistics, 1991), 5–6, 51–52, 74

Administration on Aging (AoA), 38, 75–78, 100; compendium of active grants, 102–3

Adult day care centers, 12, 13, 22–23

Alpert, Merna, 15–16

Alzheimer's disease (AD): definition 10; influence on state legislature, 46–49; respite registry, 27–29; state study committee, 38–41

Alzheimer's Disease and Related Disorders Association (ADRDA), 35–36

Americans with Disabilities Act, 103

Area Agencies on Aging (AAA), 38, 76

Arthritis Foundation, 88

Ashley, Jack, 63

Ashley, Pauline, 59–61, 118

Association for Gerontology in Higher Education, 120

Auditory Education Center, 54

Bankoff, Elizabeth, 15

Beck, John, et al., 9

Becker, Gaylene, 54

Berkow, Robert, 52, 87–88, 89

Besdine, Richard, 9, 10

Black, William and Richard Paddison, 9

Bonner, Charles, 2

Brindle, James, 106

Brown, J.H.D., 2

Burns, Eveline, 99

Califano, Joseph, 2, 106, 112, 122

Capitation payment. See Health maintenance organization (HMO)

Case management and case manager, 32, 90–91, 113, 119–20

About the Author

MERNA J. ALPERT is a diplomate as a licensed clinical social worker by the National Association of Social Workers. She is the retired executive coordinator of CAPE, a mental health program for older adults funded by the New York City Department of Mental Health, Mental Retardation, and Alcoholism Services. She also has served as adjunct assistant professor of social work at Hunter College, City University of New York. She was a mentor, at assistant professor level, at Empire State College in New York City, part of the SUNY system. She also has been a guest lecturer at Georgia State University and at Mercer University in Atlanta.